New Directions for
Community Colleges

Arthur M. Cohen
EDITOR-IN-CHIEF

Florence B. Brawer
ASSOCIATE EDITOR

Pam Schuetz
PUBLICATIONS COORDINATOR

Developing and Implementing Assessment of Student Learning Outcomes

Andreea M. Serban
Jack Friedlander
EDITORS

Number 126 • Summer 2004
Jossey-Bass
San Francisco

DEVELOPING AND IMPLEMENTING ASSESSMENT OF STUDENT LEARNING OUTCOMES
Andreea M. Serban, Jack Friedlander (eds.)
New Directions for Community Colleges, no. 126

Arthur M. Cohen, Editor-in-Chief
Florence B. Brawer, Associate Editor

Copyright © 2004 Wiley Periodicals, Inc., A Wiley Company. All rights reserved. No part of this publication may be reproduced, stored in a retrieval system, or transmitted in any form or by any means, electronic, mechanical, photocopying, recording, scanning, or otherwise, except as permitted under Sections 107 or 108 of the 1976 United States Copyright Act, without either the prior written permission of the Publisher or authorization through payment of the appropriate per-copy fee to the Copyright Clearance Center, 222 Rosewood Drive, Danvers, MA 01923, (978) 750-8400, fax (978) 646-8600. Requests to the Publisher for permission should be addressed to the Permissions Department, c/o John Wiley & Sons, Inc., 111 River St., Hoboken, NJ 07030; (201) 748-8789, fax (201) 748-6326, www.wiley.com/go/permissions.

NEW DIRECTIONS FOR COMMUNITY COLLEGES (ISSN 0194-3081, electronic ISSN 1536-0733) is part of The Jossey-Bass Higher and Adult Education Series and is published quarterly by Wiley Subscription Services, Inc., A Wiley Company, at Jossey-Bass, 989 Market Street, San Francisco, California 94103-1741. Periodicals Postage Paid at San Francisco, California, and at additional mailing offices. POSTMASTER: Send address changes to New Directions for Community Colleges, Jossey-Bass, 989 Market Street, San Francisco, California 94103-1741.

SUBSCRIPTIONS cost $80.00 for individuals and $165.00 for institutions, agencies, and libraries. Prices subject to change. See order form in back of book.

EDITORIAL CORRESPONDENCE should be sent to the Editor-in-Chief, Arthur M. Cohen, at the Graduate School of Education and Information Studies, University of California, Box 951521, Los Angeles, California 90095-1521. All manuscripts receive anonymous reviews by external referees.

New Directions for Community Colleges is indexed in Current Index to Journals in Education (ERIC).

Microfilm copies of issues and articles are available in 16mm and 35mm, as well as microfiche in 105mm, through University Microfilms Inc., 300 North Zeeb Road, Ann Arbor, Michigan 48106-1346.

Contents

Editors' Notes

As a result of changes in accreditation standards and state mandates, community colleges are under increased pressure to produce evidence of student learning and achievement. At present, many community colleges assess their effectiveness using outcome measures such as completion rates in remedial and college-level courses, persistence rates, number of degrees and certificates awarded, transfer rates, post-college earnings and, to a lesser extent, job placement rates. However, these measures of institutional effectiveness do not fully satisfy new demands for evidence of student learning. More specifically, accreditation standards and state accountability mandates are asking community colleges to produce comprehensive systems for assessing student learning outcomes that go beyond course grades, number of degrees, and certificates awarded.

Colleges are being asked to provide actual documentation of student learning at the course, program, certificate, and degree levels and to identify and measure the specific knowledge, competencies, and skills students are expected to acquire as a result of completing individual courses, general education, certificate, and degree requirements. With the exception of a few occupational programs (for example, nursing, cosmetology, and automotive technology) and industry-based certifications (for example, Cisco, Microsoft, Oracle, and Novell) that have national, state, or industry-sponsored tests that students must pass to receive a license or certificate, community colleges have not been asked by external agencies to document student learning outcomes in courses and programs until recently. As a consequence, most community colleges are not fully prepared to comply with the new demands for accountability at the outcome level of student learning.

Most of what has been written about assessment of learning outcomes has focused on four-year colleges and universities and vocational or technical programs offered at community colleges. Moreover, what has been written on this topic focuses on the rationale for assessing student learning outcomes, the processes colleges have taken or could take to implement assessment of student learning outcomes, and the identification of categories of learning outcomes that students should achieve as a result of completing institutional general education. To a much lesser extent, the literature also addresses such topics as major field requirements, observations by some faculty members that the focus on identifying and assessing learning outcomes has made them more effective teachers, and inventories of the components of a comprehensive model for assessing and improving student attainment of desired learning outcomes.

Comprehensive, practical, and sustainable models that practitioners in community college settings might use for assessing, documenting, and using information about learning outcomes to increase student attainment of desired learning outcomes are lacking at this time. Meaningful measures for assessing the learning outcomes specified by colleges are also lacking, particularly at the general education, major field, certificate, and degree levels. Moreover, there is an absence of credible evidence showing that efforts to assess student learning outcomes have resulted in gains in achieving those outcomes.

This issue of *New Directions for Community Colleges* provides a comprehensive summary of the status of the movement to assess student learning outcomes. It includes examples that community colleges can apply at the classroom, course, program, and institutional levels to satisfy local, state, and accreditation requirements for assessing learning outcomes as a means for improving student success. The volume is designed for practitioners looking for information on best practices for gaining institutional support for assessing student learning outcomes, processes to follow in designing an effective plan to assess student learning outcomes, and examples of how colleges are designing and implementing specific components of their efforts to assess student learning outcomes, particularly at the course and general education levels. This volume draws upon expertise developed at a number of community colleges in defining the desired outcomes of a general education and incorporating these desired outcomes into the assessment of student learning at the course and program levels. Challenges that practitioners have encountered in developing strategies for assessing student learning outcomes at the major field or program level are also discussed. The volume should be of interest to community college faculty, accrediting agencies, state higher education coordinating bodies, institutional researchers, policy makers, and students and faculty in higher education graduate school programs that focus on community colleges. Chapter Nine includes a number of recommendations intended for each of these audiences on roles they could play to enhance the likelihood that the desired effects for assessing student learning outcomes will in fact be achieved.

In Chapter One, Banta, Black, Kahn, and Jackson set the stage by outlining principles for good practice in planning, implementing, and sustaining community college assessment. Examples of community college approaches are provided in support of each of the principles discussed.

Serban builds on the literature of the field in Chapter Two and discusses and gives examples of concepts and major areas involved in the assessment of student learning at the institutional level. The author addresses definitions of assessment of student learning outcomes, major areas of assessment, collection and analysis of assessment data, uses of assessment, expertise and skills needed to conduct successful assessment, and cost considerations. The chapter calls for accrediting agencies, college practitioners, researchers, assessment specialists, and other state agencies to collaborate to develop integrated, practical models for identifying, assessing, measuring, and applying student learning outcomes.

In Chapter Three, Rouseff-Baker and Holm describe classroom assessment techniques that are being used as a core component of a college's efforts to assess and improve student achievement of desired learning outcomes. The chapter provides an excellent approach to engage faculty in the process of identifying, assessing, and improving student attainment of desired learning outcomes at the course and program levels. It also identifies the importance of integrating professional development efforts for faculty into the institution's strategies for assessing and improving student attainment of desired learning outcomes.

Bers deals with assessment at the program level in Chapter Four. The author argues that program-level assessments at community colleges are particularly challenging because students often achieve their goals without completing a program, or they select an array of courses that suit their needs but do not fit within an officially recognized program of study. The author provides specific examples of approaches that various community colleges are using to assess programs other than vocational and occupational ones for which licensing or certification tests developed and administered by national, state, or industry interests exist.

In Chapter Five, Burke and Minassians identify and critique performance measures used by various states to satisfy their performance-reporting requirements for community colleges. The authors make the case that reporting performance results at the state level must reflect community college missions; they provide examples and recommendations that would facilitate this goal.

In Chapter Six, Beno acquaints the reader with the context for accrediting agencies' increased emphasis on student learning outcomes as a key indicator of institutional quality and on the use of learning assessment as a key strategy for guiding institutional improvement. This chapter articulates expectations of accrediting agencies for the presentation of evidence that the institution is using student learning outcomes assessment as part of its quality improvement efforts.

In Chapter Seven, Milam, Voorhees, and Bedard-Voorhees examine policy, practice, and logistics in assessing online education. Recognizing that individuals who are disconnected from the day-to-day realities of assessing online programs most often write policy, the authors contend that policy writing should be thought-provoking for practitioners. Next the authors survey issues that drive the practice of assessing online education. The chapter concludes with assessment recommendations for institutions. Many of the issues and recommendations in this chapter apply to assessing student learning outcomes in both online and classroom-based settings.

Miles and Wilson provide an overview of the League for Innovation in the Community College's project on learning outcomes in Chapter Eight. This three-year project, which involves sixteen diverse community colleges, supported the development of practices for assessing and using student learning outcomes to improve student success. Findings from the 21st Century

Learning Outcomes Assessment Project that could be of use to other community colleges are highlighted.

Chapter Nine identifies the major challenges community colleges are facing in developing and implementing their student learning outcomes assessment efforts and offers specific suggestions for actions that can be taken by community colleges, state and accrediting agencies, and universities to facilitate the development, implementation, and continued support of student learning outcomes assessment initiatives that will increase student learning and achievement.

Although the assessment movement spans more than two decades, many community colleges are still in the early stages of their journey toward assessing student learning outcomes. The chapters in this volume are meant to facilitate and enrich this journey.

Andreea M. Serban
Jack Friedlander
Editors

Andreea M. Serban is associate vice president for information resources and director of institutional assessment, research, and planning at Santa Barbara City College in Santa Barbara, California.

Jack Friedlander is executive vice president for educational programs at Santa Barbara City College in Santa Barbara, California.

*Community colleges are increasingly pressed to develop
assessment approaches of genuine value to students,
faculty, and other stakeholders. Numerous institutional
examples illustrate a set of principles for good practice in
planning, implementing, and sustaining community
college assessment.*

A Perspective on Good Practice in Community College Assessment

*Trudy W. Banta, Karen E. Black, Susan Kahn,
Julia E. Jackson*

Americans trust higher education to serve the public in ways that other
institutions in our society cannot, but too often our citizens perceive faculty as more focused on research and other priorities within the academy
than on high-quality education for students (Massy, 2003). Alfred, Ewell,
Hudgins, and McClenney (1999) have suggested that as resources for higher
education become increasingly constrained, institutions must seek more
support than ever from external stakeholders. These authors believe that as
we seek our constituents' support, we must gain their trust by emphasizing
service, innovation, and flexibility in the education we provide.

Community college missions have long focused on educating students
for effective roles in the workforce and community as well as on providing
a variety of responsive services—the very things that Americans believe
higher education should be doing. In this sense, community colleges have
an advantage over many traditional four-year institutions in addressing the
ever more insistent calls for accountability that we have heard from external constituents since the mid-1980s. Indeed, Banta (1999) suggested that
community colleges might well be setting the standard for higher education
in using a "report-card format as a method of informing external constituents of accomplishments and progress toward goals. . . . student tracking systems, periodic and systematic employer surveys that provide one
indication of a willingness to listen to employers and other community constituents. . . . defining student success in college, and comprehensive institutional effectiveness designs" (p. 25).

Throughout this chapter examples from Mt. Hood Community College (Oregon), Midlands Technical College (South Carolina), and Sinclair Community College (Ohio), among many others, will be used to describe setting institution-wide goals and objectives for general education and transfer programs, career training and occupational retraining, remedial and developmental coursework, continuing education programs, and contract training for business and industry. These colleges each linked plans based on their goals with their budgets and with relevant measures of progress and success. They established comprehensive systems for tracking student progress, persistence, and transfer, as well as performance and satisfaction of graduates.

A New Focus on Assessing Learning

In the 1990s, as a new focus on learning began to supplant the traditional focus on teaching (Barr and Tagg, 1995), community college faculty and administrators, like their counterparts at four-year institutions, turned their attention to the assessment of learning. Early attempts to assess student learning in community colleges often relied on standardized instruments, such as the ACT Collegiate Assessment of Academic Proficiency (CAAP). Standardized tests offered a number of important advantages: they were readily available, generally presumed to be reliable and valid, and yielded scores that could be compared with those of students at peer institutions.

However, faculty at community colleges, like colleagues at four-year institutions, frequently found such instruments to be of limited value in capturing useful information about student learning. Standardized tests are usually administered outside the regular curriculum and thus tend to be detached from the genuine interests and priorities of both students and faculty. Students may lack motivation to do their best on tests that have no real consequences for them, while many faculty tend to view standardized tests as unrelated to the kinds of learning that concern them most. While many community colleges do continue to make use of standardized tests, approaches embedded in ongoing course work are more likely to elicit students' best efforts and thus to yield genuinely useful information for improving curriculum, pedagogy, and, ultimately, student learning (Seybert, 2002).

Recognizing the weaknesses of standardized testing, faculty at a number of community colleges have begun to align assessment approaches with locally developed, campus-specific goals for student learning and accomplishment. Such approaches often rely on performance-based assessment methodologies, such as portfolios, capstone projects, and internship experiences. Butler Community College (Kansas) offers an illustration of an ongoing, systematic assessment program for general education. Faculty develop their own course-based assignments designed to assess specific desired outcomes of the general education curriculum, such as critical thinking skills (Speary, 2001). Students complete these assignments, including open-ended questions, papers, and speeches, as part of their regular class work and receive grades on them. During the following semester, samples of the student work are analyzed by interdisciplinary groups of faculty, using a common scoring rubric. Findings are submitted to an assessment team that aggregates the data and reports institution-wide results. These data are, in turn, discussed and further analyzed in departmental faculty meetings. Administrators and students have opportunities to review the data as well.

During the third semester of the assessment cycle, the director of assessment and a faculty representative from the assessment team meet with faculty and administrators to review findings and discuss needed improvements in curriculum, planning, budgeting, or the assessment process. To begin the next cycle, the director of assessment identifies for each department the courses from which samples of student work will be drawn. Faculty then generate the assignments that will be assessed, and the process continues.

Embedding the assessment process in individual courses has dramatically increased enthusiasm for assessment at Butler among students and faculty alike (Speary, 2002). In addition, the cyclical nature of the process assures that assessment and improvement efforts are coherent and ongoing, rather than scattered and sporadic. Butler provides just one example of the many community colleges that are engaged in a range of effective assessment practices. Rather than attempting a comprehensive overview of assessment in community colleges, this chapter will identify a set of principles of good practice in assessment, and then describe initiatives at several institutions that illustrate these principles.

Principles of Good Practice

Two decades of experience with outcomes assessment at hundreds of institutions across the country has prompted development of several lists of principles of good practice. One of the first of these lists was compiled by a group of assessment scholars convened by the American Association for Higher Education (AAHE) (Hutchings, 1993). Later, Banta, Lund, Black, and Oblander (1996) illustrated and expanded on the AAHE list. In 2002, Banta drew on these and other statements to develop a more detailed set of principles characterizing good practice in three phases of assessment: planning, implementing, and improving and sustaining. These principles are summarized here and illustrated with examples drawn from assessment practice at community colleges across the country.

Planning. Effective practice in outcomes assessment begins with a planning phase that may be characterized by the following four principles:

Involves stakeholders (faculty, administrators, students, student affairs professionals, employers, community representatives) from the outset to incorporate their needs and interests and solicit later support.

Begins when the need is recognized; allows sufficient time for development—timing is crucial.
Has a written plan with clear purposes that are related to goals people value
and to a larger set of conditions that promote change. Assessment is a
vehicle for improvement, not an end in itself.
Bases assessment approaches on clear, explicitly stated program objectives
(Banta, 2002).

If assessment is to result in genuine improvement, those who will be
implementing assessment approaches and making use of assessment findings must be engaged in developing objectives, plans, and processes related
to educational goals to which they are truly committed. In community college settings, involving community representatives, including potential
employers of students as well as campus stakeholders, is especially important. Efforts to engage these external and internal stakeholders must begin
early and persist. Collaboration among these groups to define goals and
strategies and to articulate agreed-upon learning objectives in clear, measurable ways sets the stage for smooth implementation, provides a basis for
analyzing and using findings for improvement, and helps ensure that assessment efforts will be sustained.

One model for involving important external stakeholders is illustrated
by Owens Community College (Ohio), where the Industrial and Engineering Technologies division has developed corporate partnerships with area
employers to advance several majors (Devier, 2002). Partners participate
with faculty in developing learning outcome statements for relevant majors,
such as Transportation Technologies, and contribute to the assessment process by evaluating the performance of students involved in field experiences
at partner sites. Faculty use these evaluations, in conjunction with campus-
based assessment findings, to recommend needed adjustments to curriculum, objectives, or measures. In the Owens example, consideration of
specific stakeholder priorities for student learning from the outset of planning for assessment shaped subsequent stages of the process and led to the
use of authentic assessment approaches firmly embedded in the curriculum—in this case, assessment of student work in field experiences.

St. Charles Community College (Missouri) provides another example
of the successful involvement of stakeholders in producing assessment measures and strategies focused on specific program goals. There a faculty-led
process replaced an administration-led assessment initiative that relied on
standardized tests. Faculty developed written goals and objectives for student learning in writing, oral communication, math and science, social science and the humanities, and computer literacy. Within each of these areas,
faculty designed "assessment projects" tailored to the goals and objectives,
with measures based on authentic student work in designated classes. As St.
Charles faculty applied findings from the projects and realized visible gains
in student learning and success within both developmental and general

education courses, faculty interest and participation in assessment greatly increased. The success of the initial assessment cycles using the new process spurred new projects and the model became the basis for St. Charles's ongoing assessment efforts (Jones, Banks, and Gray, 2003; St. Charles Community College, 2001).

Mt. Hood Community College (Oregon) is another exemplar of systematic planning and assessment that bring together the entire college community. Following a 1997 accreditation review that advised the campus to devote greater attention to long-term planning, the president charged a strategic planning council with designing and coordinating a planning process. The approach included input from key stakeholders at every stage. For example, in the initial stage of planning, the college gathered information on anticipated needs from faculty, staff, local employers, and campus forums open to staff and community members. As the plan began to take shape, members of the strategic planning council conducted surveys and focus groups with area employers, made presentations and sought input from a range of community groups, and visited the college's divisions and departments to gather feedback and identify high-priority faculty needs. Throughout the process, budget allocations were explicitly aligned with planning priorities (Mt. Hood Community College, 2001).

As the Mt. Hood plan neared completion, a collegewide forum was held that focused specifically on the college's mission and primary purposes. By fall 2001, the college had adopted a new mission that included statements of vision and core values, along with five major areas of focus: knowledge-based workforce; access and diversity; requirements of economic development; transitions (for example, transfer and job placement); and student success. Indicators developed for each area of focus include both academic and facilities needs and emphasize ongoing input from all stakeholders. For example, the indicators for "knowledge-based workforce" include faculty participation in and satisfaction with professional development activities and employer feedback on the college's customized training services. Access and diversity indicators include the extent to which employee and student profiles of protected classes—including children, pregnant women, prisoners, people with handicaps, and people with mental disabilities—approximated the community profile. Meeting program development and enrollment targets served as one indicator for economic development. One transition indicator is job placement of graduates. And finally, student satisfaction with the college is an indicator for student success. Broad campus participation and the integration of strategic planning, budget allocation, and improvement activities have resulted in widespread commitment to ongoing improvement, to campus mission, and to student success (Mt. Hood Community College, 2001).

Implementing. Effective assessment practice depends on implementation of a carefully planned design. Successful implementation has the following characteristics:

Has knowledgeable, effective leadership.

Recognizes that assessment is essential to learning and is therefore the shared responsibility of everyone at the institution.

Includes faculty and staff development to prepare individuals to implement assessment and use the findings.

Devolves responsibility for assessment to the unit level.

Recognizes that learning is multidimensional and developmental and thus uses multiple measures to maximize reliability and validity.

Assesses processes as well as outcomes.

Occurs in an environment that is receptive, supportive, and enabling—on a continuing basis.

Incorporates continuous communication with constituents concerning activities and findings. Effective outcomes assessment produces data that guide improvement on a continuing basis (Banta, 2002).

Genuinely useful assessment programs are deeply embedded in institutional culture. Such programs are built on a foundation of sustained, committed leadership; an understanding that effective assessment is essential to learning; and a sense that the responsibility for learning and assessment is shared by everyone at the institution. A supportive environment for assessment marshals the necessary resources, including faculty and staff development, to implement sound assessment approaches. For assessment to succeed, findings must be interpreted clearly and applied to an ongoing improvement cycle that is widely visible to stakeholders, both internal and external.

Some community college campuses have found that technology can be an invaluable tool for supporting and communicating about assessment. At Sinclair Community College, faculty have created guiding principles for assessment, such as "Assessment of student learning and development is a process that is separate from faculty evaluation." Using such principles, faculty in each department determine specific approaches and methods that they will use to assess student learning and development. A database on the college Web site serves as a tool for sharing and leveraging successes, ideas, lessons learned, and recommendations for improvement. All Sinclair stakeholders—including faculty and staff, current students, graduates, and employers, as well as other educational institutions—are encouraged to submit ideas and materials to the site. The site has helped to improve communication within the campus, to strengthen the sense of shared responsibility for assessment, and to document for stakeholders the Sinclair journey toward using assessment findings to improve campus practices and outcomes (Sinclair Community College, 2003a).

Assessment experts recognize that if assessment is to improve learning, then processes and practices as well as outcomes must be assessed. Indeed, Ewell (2002) has observed that institutions frequently begin assessment as part of initiatives to implement new instructional or curricular approaches, such as service learning or writing across the curriculum. At Lane Community College (Oregon), a "Strategic Learning Initiative" focuses on using new knowledge about the nature of learning to shape experiments with learning communities, enhancements to the college's technology infrastructure, alternative course schedules and formats, distance education, and a variety of faculty development projects. From the outset, assessment has been viewed as intrinsic to this initiative. The aims of the initiative include fostering faculty expertise in assessment, assessing the effectiveness of the various projects within the initiative for improving learning, and using the results of assessment to identify needed refinements to the projects (Lane Community College, 2003).

Similarly, when the Metropolitan Community College District of Kansas City implemented a learning community initiative, faculty quickly realized that multiple types of assessment data, both quantitative and qualitative, would need to be collected and analyzed, using multiple methods, if they were to understand the impact of the initiative on student learning and to make any needed adjustments. The variety of methods they adopted focused on learning processes (how students were learning) as well as on outcomes, and included both formative and summative approaches. For example, structured interviews with students and faculty in the program elicited reflections on both learning and teaching experiences in learning communities. Classroom observations examined group dynamics as a basis for analyzing how interaction between students and faculty contributes to student learning. Students took a pre- and post-survey on attitudes toward specific types of learning experiences, as well as standardized tests designed to measure general education outcomes (Van Middlesworth, 2003).

Improving and Sustaining. Adhering to the principles of planning and implementation discussed above helps to ensure that a credible assessment process will be put in place. But even effective assessment practice can always be improved. Indeed, an improvement phase is essential to sustaining outcomes assessment over time. In this phase, a successful assessment process does the following:

Produces credible evidence of learning and organizational effectiveness.
Ensures that assessment data are used to improve programs and services.
Provides a vehicle for demonstrating accountability to stakeholders.
Encompasses the expectation that outcomes assessment will be ongoing, not episodic.
Incorporates ongoing evaluation and improvement of the assessment process itself (Banta, 2002).

Unfortunately, credible evidence of learning and effectiveness can be elusive; it is for this reason that most assessment experts advocate the use of multiple assessment measures and sources of information. For example, combining direct evidence of learning from standardized tests with student work produced within the regular curriculum or co-curriculum and indirect evidence from sources such as student surveys and focus groups provides a more complete picture of learning than single measures alone. Beyond interpreting evidence and its implications for improvement, faculty and staff must engage in collective consideration of the quality of the evidence and of the processes for developing and collecting that evidence, making changes when these seem warranted. Proponents of reflective practice have long held that this "second look" at assessment practices is necessary to complete a current assessment cycle, to improve the effectiveness of the next cycle, and to sustain the vitality of an assessment initiative (Banta, 2002).

Sinclair Community College has focused specifically on developing processes for sustaining assessment. Assessment began at Sinclair in the late 1980s, when the college first developed learning outcomes. The college has maintained a commitment to assessment through to the present, continuing not only to assess desired learning outcomes, but also to focus on what it takes to continue and sustain this commitment (Sinclair Community College, 2003b). For example, the college was careful to be inclusive in developing initial plans for assessment and, in the implementation phase, created administrative and faculty governance structures that helped institutionalize assessment. Factors that contributed to wide participation and a supportive environment for implementing assessment included awards to faculty who had contributed to assessment efforts, grants to departments to support assessment projects, and empowerment of departments to establish learning outcomes, design assessment instruments, and determine needed improvements based on assessment findings.

The Sinclair Web site includes annual assessment reports from each department and documents the benefits of assessment in alerting faculty to areas, such as advising, where changes were clearly needed and which, once in place, have contributed to student learning. Wise planning and implementation, along with a purposive approach to using assessment findings for improvement and to communicating assessment activities and results, have all helped to make assessment an ongoing feature of the campus culture at Sinclair.

Lane Community College also has conducted research on its assessment activities. Three faculty members developed case studies that described and detailed assessment efforts at the department level. Using in-depth interviews, the researchers studied the status of assessment efforts in each department and gathered information on barriers and incentives associated with faculty participation in assessment. Barriers included the perception of assessment as a one-time summative activity or "end product," rather than as a means to the ends of improved learning and effectiveness, as well as fears that faculty time and effort would be wasted if assessment were to be dropped as a campus priority in the future. Incentives included an understanding of assessment as an ongoing, cyclical process, intrinsic to effective

teaching and learning, and use of assessment practices that are clearly beneficial to all concerned—students, faculty, administrators, and employers. In
addition, the researchers at Lane recommended wider reporting of assessment findings and results and further study aimed at encouraging faculty
participation in order to sustain assessment work (Berger, Kluber, and
Schubert, 1998).

We noted above the importance of credible evidence for improving and
sustaining assessment. To date, however, community colleges and their
stakeholders have not resolved the issue of what constitutes credible evidence of effectiveness in all areas of their missions. For example, the transfer function of community colleges is an area where the "evidence" has been
especially confusing, in large part because varied definitions of transfer have
produced widely divergent findings on community college transfer rates.
Seybert noted in 1994 that several national efforts were under way to
"define and calculate a national transfer rate" (p. 29). One of those, a panel
convened in December 1994 and again in 1999, developed a set of indicators of effectiveness for community colleges, including those for the transfer function (Alfred and others, 1999). However, Townsend (2002), among
others, has argued that we have yet to agree on a common definition of
transfer. Changing student attendance patterns, such as the phenomenon
of student "swirling"—moving back and forth between multiple colleges—
exacerbate this definitional problem (de los Santos and Wright, 1990;
Association of American Colleges and Universities, 2002).

Clearer evidence and choices are available to those assessing general
education and other areas of the community college mission. Indeed, some
community colleges have become exemplars on the basis of their effective
use of evidence. For St. Charles, as for most community colleges, improving the success of students in developmental studies courses was a high priority. To gauge the impact of developmental writing courses, faculty
instituted a common, holistically scored final exam for students in developmental writing sections. Comparison of these final essays with the essays
students had written for initial placement led English department faculty to
revise the placement criteria as well as the curricula for the developmental
classes. As a result of the changes, the effectiveness of developmental writing courses has improved to the point that students now pass the freshman-
level course at the same rates as students who placed directly into that
course (Jones, Banks, and Gray, 2003; St. Charles, 2001).

Midlands Technical Community College has developed an institutional
effectiveness initiative as a strategy for ongoing institutional renewal and as
a means to demonstrate that its performance matches its purposes (Banta,
1999). A comprehensive planning and evaluation process identified six areas
critical to institutional effectiveness: accessible, comprehensive programs of
high quality; student satisfaction and retention; post-education satisfaction
and success; economic development and community involvement; sound,
effective resource management; and dynamic organizational involvement and

development. Within these areas, twenty performance indicators were identified, all reflecting the college's core commitment to student success.

Now Midlands uses several vehicles to communicate regularly with stakeholders about progress in achieving the benchmarks established for each indicator of effectiveness. Some programs, for example, ask members of the local business community to serve on program review teams, as a way of communicating with essential stakeholders and also learning from them. Assessment results for each indicator of effectiveness are communicated through a variety of published reports, including an Institutional Effectiveness Report Card, which is a detailed update on progress toward objectives submitted annually to the institution's board of trustees (Banta, 1999).

Effective assessment poses an ongoing challenge to educational institutions at all levels. Community colleges have a special responsibility to keep pace with changes in the nature of the college-going population and with evolving societal and economic needs. Carrying out this responsibility demands, in turn, a willingness to engage continuously in experimentation and innovation in curricula and in teaching and learning. Assessment is an essential component of any effective approach to fulfilling these commitments to responsiveness and flexibility. We must inquire continuously into whether our programs are meeting student and other stakeholder needs, and we must assess educational innovations to ensure that they are resulting in the learning students require. We believe that attention to the principles and exemplars discussed in this chapter, to a campuswide commitment to student learning, to success in achieving institutional mission, and to authentic accountability will help community colleges to develop assessment approaches of genuine value to students, faculty, and stakeholders alike.

References

Alfred, R., Ewell, P., Hudgins, J., and McClenney, K. *Core Indicators of Effectiveness for Community Colleges.* Washington, D.C.: Community College Press, 1999.

Association of American Colleges and Universities. *Greater Expectations, A New Vision for Learning as a Nation Goes to College.* Washington, D.C.: Association of American Colleges and Universities, 2002.

Banta, T. W. *Assessment in Community Colleges: Setting the Standard for Higher Education?* Boulder, Colo.: National Center for Higher Education Management Systems, 1999.

Banta, T. W. "Characteristics of Effective Outcomes Assessment—Foundations and Examples." In T. W. Banta and Associates (eds.), *Building a Scholarship of Assessment.* San Francisco: Jossey-Bass, 2002.

Banta, T. W., Lund, J. P., Black, K. E., and Oblander, F. W. *Assessment in Practice: Putting Principles to Work on College Campuses.* San Francisco: Jossey-Bass, 1996.

Barr, R. B., and Tagg, J. "From Teaching to Learning—A New Paradigm for Undergraduate Education." *Change,* 1995, 27(6), 12–25.

Berger, D., Kluber, A., and Schubert, M. *Program Assessment: A Case Study Approach.* Eugene, Oreg.: Lane Community College, 1998.

de los Santos, A., and Wright, I. "Maricopa's Swirling Students: Earning One-Third of Arizona State's Bachelor's Degrees." *Community, Technical, and Junior College Journal,* 1990, *60*(6), 32–34.

Devier, D. H. "Corporate Partnership Student Assessment: The Owens Community College Experience." *Assessment Update,* 2002, *14*(5), 8–10.

Ewell, P. T. "An Emerging Scholarship: A Brief History of Assessment." In T. W. Banta and Associates (eds.), *Building a Scholarship of Assessment.* San Francisco: Jossey-Bass, 2002.

Hutchings, P. "Principles of Good Practice for Assessing Student Learning." *Assessment Update,* 1993, *5*(1), 6–7.

Jones, K., Banks, M. L., and Gray, J. "The Road Not Taken: An Assessment Program Where Everyone Wins." *A Collection of Papers on Self-Study and Institutional Improvement.* Chicago: The Higher Learning Commission, North Central Association of Schools and Colleges, 2003.

Lane Community College. "Strategic Learning Initiative: Goals and Initiatives." http://teach.lanecc.edu/sli/slig&o.htm. Accessed Dec. 19, 2003.

Massy, W. F. *Honoring the Trust: Quality and Cost Containment in Higher Education.* Boston: Anker Publishing, 2003.

Mt. Hood Community College. "Mt. Hood Community College Education Plan, Part I." Gresham, Oreg.: Mt. Hood Community College, 2001. http://www.mhcc.edu/campus/campus_info/allabout/research/institutional_master_plan/education/main.htm. Accessed Dec. 18, 2003.

Seybert, J. A. "Assessment from a National Perspective: Where Are We, Really?" In T. H. Bers and M. L. Mittler (eds.), *Assessment and Testing: Myths and Realities.* New Directions for Community Colleges, no. 88. San Francisco: Jossey-Bass, 1994.

Seybert, J. A. "Assessing Student Learning Outcomes." In T. H. Bers and H. D. Calhoun (eds.), *Next Steps for the Community College.* New Directions for Community Colleges, no. 117. San Francisco: Jossey-Bass, 2002.

Sinclair Community College. "Assessment of Student Learning: Guiding Principles." http://www.sinclair.edu/about/assessment/principles/index.cfm. Accessed Dec. 19, 2003a.

Sinclair Community College. "Assessment of Student Learning: Assessment of Student Learning." http://www.sinclair.edu/about/assessment/index.cfm. Accessed Dec. 19, 2003b.

Speary, P. "Community College Strategies—Collegewide Assessment of General Education: The Butler County Community College Model." *Assessment Update,* 2001, *13*(6), 12–13.

Speary, P. "Community College Strategies—The Butler County Community College Individualized Student Assessment Pilot Project." *Assessment Update,* 2002, *14*(3), 8–9, 11.

St. Charles Community College. "Accreditation Self-Study Report for the Higher Learning Commission of the North Central Association," 2001. http://www.stchas.edu/NCA/10.pdf. Accessed Dec. 18, 2003.

Townsend, B. K. "Transfer Rates: A Problematic Criterion for Measuring the Community College." In T. H. Bers and H. D. Calhoun (eds.), *Next Steps for the Community College.* New Directions for Community Colleges, no. 117. San Francisco: Jossey-Bass, 2002.

Van Middlesworth, C. "Community College Strategies: Assessing Learning Communities." *Assessment Update,* 2003, *15*(2), 12–13, 15–16.

TRUDY W. BANTA *is vice-chancellor for planning and institutional improvement at Indiana University-Purdue University Indianapolis.*

KAREN E. BLACK *is assistant to the vice-chancellor for planning and institutional improvement at Indiana University-Purdue University Indianapolis.*

SUSAN KAHN *is director of the Office of Institutional Effectiveness at Indiana University-Purdue University Indianapolis.*

JULIA E. JACKSON *is a graduate assistant for planning and institutional improvement at Indiana University-Purdue University Indianapolis.*

2

While the assessment movement has spanned more than two decades, there is great variation in its degree of implementation among community colleges throughout the country. Building on literature in the field, this chapter discusses and gives examples of concepts and major areas involved in the assessment of student learning at the institutional level.

Assessment of Student Learning Outcomes at the Institutional Level

Andreea M. Serban

Education literature provides various definitions of assessment. Palomba and Banta (1999) define it this way: "Assessment is the systematic collection, review, and use of information about educational programs undertaken for the purpose of improving student learning and development" (p. 4). Volkwein (2003) gives a more specific definition: "Student outcomes assessment is the act of assembling and analyzing both qualitative and quantitative teaching and learning outcomes evidence in order to examine their congruence with an institution's stated purposes and educational objectives" (p. 4).

Assessment of student learning outcomes in community colleges typically involves measurement of student performance at the levels of course, program, and institution. Chapter Three discusses some examples of course-level assessment techniques and Chapter Four addresses the challenges of program-level assessment in community colleges. This chapter focuses on assessment of student learning outcomes at the institutional level, and it gives supporting examples from community college practice. This chapter also addresses the types of skills needed to conduct assessment as well as considerations related to the cost of assessment.

Educational Purposes and Learning Objectives

Effective assessment begins with clear, overall institutional goals and values. Goals and values are found in the institutional mission of almost every college, and they should clarify what an institution plans and hopes to do.

As Volkwein (2003) states, "First, just as articulating educational objectives is a necessary first step in measuring student academic attainment, articulating institutional purposes is a necessary first step in demonstrating organizational effectiveness" (p. 5). Overall institutional values and goals become operational through more specific goals and objectives captured in college short- and long-term plans. Measures of student learning and achievement should be integrated into the objectives included in institutional plans.

Educational Purposes and Institutional Assessment

Volkwein (2003) suggests that the following areas of educational activity have distinct importance for linking purposes, resources, and educational outcomes: basic skills (developmental or remedial) education, general education, major, and students' personal and social development. Since Chapter Four discusses assessment at the program and major level, this area is not addressed in this chapter.

Basic Skills. Basic skills education has two major purposes: to correct students' educational deficiencies in order to prepare them for college-level work, and to help students transition into college-level courses. Community colleges enroll the majority of students requiring basic skills (Keup, 1998). A 2000 survey conducted by the National Center for Education Statistics found that 42 percent of first-time freshmen enrolled in community colleges in fall 2000 took basic skills courses in reading, writing, or mathematics (2003).

Assessment of basic skills is clearly more than the placement testing or initial student assessment that most community colleges conduct. Assessment of basic skills needs to include exit proficiencies and tracking of students' transition and performance in college-level courses. Such an assessment should include comparisons between performance in college-level courses of students who transitioned from basic skills versus students who did not need remedial education (cognitive assessment). In addition, as noted by Volkwein (2003), self-reported measures of attitude, satisfaction, and goal completion provide information about non-cognitive factors, which may have significant impact on the outcomes of the learning process.

Community colleges have adopted various interventions and approaches to assess basic skills courses and programs. South Suburban College (Illinois) adopted a structured model in the early 1990s that demonstrates that intrusive procedures need not be punitive and can actually foster a caring environment for students with remedial needs (Yamasaki, 1998). Samples of the fourteen policies of the model include mandatory placement testing for full-time and part-time students who have taken six credit hours, mandating basic skills courses beginning with the student's first semester, and requiring students on academic warning or probation status to develop an action plan to improve their academic standing.

The San Diego Community College District instituted mandatory enforcement of all course prerequisites, including recommended levels of English and math skills (Yamasaki, 1998). Previously, the district did not insist upon enforcement of prerequisites, and students often enrolled in courses that were inappropriate for their ability levels. Some of the positive outcomes of this approach include increases in instructional research conducted by faculty as well as interaction among colleagues across the district.

Collaborative partnerships between community colleges and their feeder high schools are effective in reducing the need for postsecondary basic skills education (Yamasaki, 1998). By developing a secondary-school writing curriculum and an assessment system that relies heavily on portfolios that follow students throughout high school and to the community college, faculty from the two educational segments can make significant strides in promoting student success. Such a model also addresses growing public concerns that basic skills courses in higher education are simply repeating what students should have learned in high school.

Other community colleges have implemented computer-aided instruction systems and associated assessment models to improve the students' success in basic skills. Canada's Nova Scotia Community College System implemented the INVEST system, which incorporates approximately four thousand lessons into a three-tiered system. Tier 1 provides Literacy-Based Instruction, Tier 2 focuses on Adult Basic Education, and Tier 3 furnishes General Education Development (GED) Exam Preparation. Mathematics, reading, writing, and life-skills instruction are available in each of the three tiers, and instructors determine the level of mastery required for students to progress within the tier (Keup, 1998). Instructors also communicate with students through a computerized journal. One file of the journal is private, and students are encouraged to write in it daily. The other file is an interactive teacher-student journal. Students are expected to write comments, concerns, and questions on a daily basis, and the instructor reads and responds to the student communications.

According to Wilson (1992) and Moore (1993), student gains using the INVEST system were achieved in both reading and math. The increase in reading scores was not significantly different from the gains found in reading among students in a traditional, non-computerized basic skills program. However, the increase in mathematics achievement, particularly in the areas of mathematical concepts and problem solving, was greater than the gains in classrooms using traditional teaching approaches.

Project SYNERGY is an instructional management system that was developed through the efforts of nineteen two-year colleges and three four-year colleges under the direction of Miami-Dade Community College (Florida). The system and instructional software are the result of research conducted by thirty-nine faculty members at four institutions. They reviewed more than 298 software packages to assess quality, amass a bank of questions to test for basic skills mastery, and conduct software implementation tests

(Anandam, 1994). The end product of the review is the Project SYNERGY integrator, an adaptive, computerized management system for basic skills education (Anandam, 1994).

The Project SYNERGY Integrator (PSI) facilitates basic skills development through a Windows-driven access module for the student and command module for the instructor. The integration of these two modules allows instructors to set preferences, monitor the students' progress, receive reports, modify the curriculum, send e-mail, and personally intervene in the learning process. In addition, through the system, the student is able to create a personalized curriculum based on computerized placement tests. The student is also able to ask for assistance from other students or the instructor at any time during the learning process.

A pretest determines where students are placed initially within the lessons in each subject area. These computerized lessons provide information and opportunities for practice in the four subject areas. Posttests measure students' mastery of the subjects. A successful performance on the posttest allows the student to advance to the next module of pretest and to lessons in that tier. Instructors are made aware of student difficulties through a "lock out" mechanism on the program. That is, after the maximum number of unsuccessful attempts (as previously determined by the instructor) is reached on the mastery tests, the program will freeze and require the student to see the instructor in order to continue the program (Moore, 1993).

General Education. Palomba and Banta (1999) state: "An essential aim [of general education] is to activate the verbal, numerical, and visual skills necessary to analyze and synthesize information, construct arguments, and identify and solve problems" (p. 242). The broad competencies that are the subject of assessment related to general education include cognitive abilities (critical thinking, problem solving), content literacy (knowledge of social institutions, science, and technology), literacy skills (communication, information skills), and value awareness (multicultural understanding, moral and ethical judgment) (Volkwein, 2003; see Chapter Eight in this volume for additional detail).

Palomba and Banta (1999) suggest three different types of approaches to assessment of general education: individual course-based approach, multicourse (theme-based) approach, and non-course-based approach. These approaches are not mutually exclusive. In the individual course-based approach, assessment information is collected about the learning that occurs in individual courses in relation to one or more general education goals. In the multicourse approach, faculty from a number of disciplines may be asked to provide evidence that certain learning objectives are being met in their courses. Learning communities are examples of multicourse approaches. Non-course-based approaches are campuswide and focus on individuals or groups of students rather than courses.

Methods and instruments for assessment of general education include standardized tests, self-reported measures of progress obtained through locally developed or published surveys, essays, class discussions, class exit assignments, course-embedded assessment activities, portfolios, and capstone courses. Assessments of general education may also include reviews of course syllabi and inventories of class assignments (Palomba and Banta, 1999).

Community colleges have engaged in assessment of general education with varied degrees of success. For example, Northern Virginia Community College used an internal program review process "to assess aspects of the cross-disciplinary general education, including student outcomes. Assessment methods include common final exams, student projects and assignments, portfolios, and videotapes. A review of findings has produced change in course objectives and content, methods of instruction, and library resources" (Robertson and Simpson, 1996, p. 190).

Guided by the literature describing assessment and good teaching practices, which suggests that course syllabi can be used as indicators of student learning outcomes, a group from Oakton Community College (Illinois) analyzed the content of course syllabi for 114 fall 1995 social science courses and 135 Spring 1997 social science and business courses (Bers, Davis, and Taylor, 2000). The analysis was based on a coding system that took into consideration, among many other aspects, overall learning objectives and the topics to be covered. The analysis found that many syllabi "failed to contain clear information about the amount of required reading and writing, types of tests or other assignments, definitions of class participations, components of the final grade and their weights in the final grade calculation, or dates for tests and assignments" (p. 5). In addition to the syllabi analysis, a student survey was conducted in order to determine what items students saw as important for course syllabi and to examine whether they found syllabi to be generally adequate. The results from the course syllabus analysis and the student survey were used as a basis for professional development and faculty workshops.

Students' Personal and Social Development. Community colleges serve an important role in the personal and social development of students. Student services such as advising, tutoring, counseling, financial aid, and services for students with disabilities, or educational opportunity services for low-income students all influence the personal and social development of students. Personal development outcomes include self-awareness and self-reliance, awareness of values, interpersonal relations, and leadership qualities (Volkwein, 2003).

The assessment techniques most frequently used to assess growth in students' personal and social development include surveys, interviews, and focus groups. Instruments readily available to facilitate assessment in this area include the National Survey of Student Engagement and the College Student Experiences Survey. The cost of administering such instruments may be prohibitive for smaller community colleges, in which case locally developed instruments may be a better alternative.

Regardless of the purpose and level, assessments should be scrutinized by the following criteria:

Utility: does the assessment serve practical information needs?
Feasibility: is the assessment realistic and prudent?
Propriety: does the assessment conform to legal and ethical standards?
Accuracy: is the assessment technically adequate?
(Davis, 1989, p. 18)

Reporting and Using Assessment Results

One of the primary purposes of assessment is to improve teaching and learning. Improvement can occur if adequate, timely, and systematic feedback is provided to all who are involved in assessment, including faculty, students, counselors, and administrators. However, as Astin (1993) notes, "[Since] most practitioners have no means to connect their specific actions to student progress and development, it is difficult for them to know whether the environments they create are having their intended effects on student outcomes" (p. 128). Thus, the reporting of assessment results should allow for feedback and facilitation of the practitioners' understanding of the linkage between their actions, the environment, and student outcomes. In other words, assessment should facilitate explanation of causal relationships between various policies, practices, methods, and specified student outcomes.

Assessment results are most effectively utilized in practice if they are designed specifically for particular audiences (Ewell, 1987). Communicating assessment results to faculty, students, student services staff, and administrators, respectively, should focus on the aspects of greatest interest to each group (Astin, 1993). For example, faculty are most interested in the courses they teach, the instructional and pedagogical methods they use, and the educational climate of the department in which they teach. Student services staff are most interested in the impact of services they provide. As such, assessment results related to student satisfaction with these services as well as student achievement measures (for example, retention and successful course and degree completion) would be most relevant for this group. For administrators, results aggregated at the program and institutional levels would be of most interest. Aggregated results for major areas such as basic skills and general education are also of interest. Comparisons across departments and against peer institutions (where data are available) constitute another area of interest. Students, on the other hand, tend to be most interested in data describing individual courses and instructors, programs or majors, and special programs (such as basic skills, counseling, tutoring), as well as aggregated results by age, gender, and ethnic groups. Retention, satisfaction, and job placement are among the outcomes that students seek when making decisions about their undergraduate education.

Regional and professional accrediting agencies and state higher education coordinating agencies are another type of audience with different interests. Currently, all regional accrediting agencies require member institutions to collect and use assessment of student learning outcomes for improvement, decision making, planning, and resource allocation. As noted in Chapter Six, accrediting agencies expect evidence of engagement in assessment of student learning outcomes at all institutional levels: course, program, institution, and across instructional and student services programs. Professional accreditors also emphasize student learning outcomes and, particularly, demonstration of performance in specific competency and skills areas.

Most states currently require periodic reporting on performance indicators that emphasize student achievement rather than student learning outcomes. Regardless of the form of presentation and communication, the utilization of assessment results has little impact without the strong support of the administration. Also, the importance of assessment results is diminished in the absence of any linkage to internal processes such as program review, planning, and budgeting.

Assessment Expertise and Skills

One of the major challenges in building, sustaining, and effectively utilizing student learning outcomes assessment is having the needed expertise and skills on campus. Astin (1993) asserts that "lack of expertise is a major impediment to the effective use of assessment in American higher education" (p. 140). He further states that many colleges have faculty and staff conversant in the different fields on which assessment is based (such as testing, measurement, statistics, learning theory, curriculum, planning, and research design). However, lack of knowledge about assessment processes and tools was identified as a key reason for the difficulties faced by some of the colleges involved in the 21st Century Learning Outcomes Assessment Project (see Chapter Eight). As early as 1985, Ewell argued that involvement of faculty and administrators does not guarantee the success of any assessment program. It is the right mix of expertise and skills of the individuals involved in developing the assessment framework of an institution that plays a critical role in successful assessment efforts.

Campuses must ensure that they involve individual experts or groups that have the combined expertise and skills in the various fields relevant to assessment. Discussed below are several critical qualifications for an ideal assessment expert (Astin, 1993).

Vision. A broad and comprehensive grasp of institutional goals and purposes combined with a clear view of how assessment processes and outcomes can be used to advance these goals and purposes is a key qualification. Whereas presidents and vice presidents, particularly those in academic affairs or instruction, have the broad and comprehensive understanding of institutional goals and purposes, they might not have a similar under-standing of how best to use assessment in relationship to institutional goals and purposes. The time realistically needed for assessment training and the demands placed on these administrators by their primary responsibilities may not allow them to acquire an extensive view of assessment processes and outcomes. Generally, by the nature of their work and interaction with all units of a college, individuals doing institutional assessment, research, and planning are well positioned to have or more quickly develop the vision that Astin suggests.

Understanding of the college. A clear conceptual understanding of how colleges function and of the strengths and limitations of faculty and administrators as they perform their individual and collective roles within the college is needed. Such understanding assumes having worked in a par-ticular college for some time as well as systematic interaction with the aca-demic and service units of the college.

Functional knowledge. A thorough knowledge of measurement the-ory, statistical methods (especially multivariate statistics), and research design is also needed. Astin underscores the importance of having "func-tional" knowledge, which means the ability to facilitate the implementation of useful assessment methods, processes and outcomes, and procedures of data analysis.

Technical know-how. Individuals doing institutional assessment and research should possess practical knowledge of techniques of data collec-tion; data organization, storage, and retrieval; and data analysis. Depending on their level of skills, they may need assistance from a computer pro-grammer.

Understanding of relevant concepts. Understanding and knowledge of learning theory, instructional methods and theory, curriculum, support services, student development theory, and group dynamics are also critical. In community colleges, the likelihood of one individual being conversant in all these areas is quite low. However, a group of administrators and fac-ulty from various disciplines could be assembled whose collective expertise encompasses these diverse educational and social sciences concepts.

Good communication skills. The ideal assessment expert has the ability to listen, speak, and write clearly as well as the ability to express complex ideas and findings in accurate, concise, and persuasive terms.

Academic qualifications. According to Astin (1993), an assessment expert should have training, experience, and accomplishments comparable to those needed for appointment to a tenure-track faculty position. Clearly, he is referring to four-year institutions, where a record of extensive publi-cations and research is an important factor for such appointments. In com-munity colleges, faculty are not required to publish or conduct research in order to receive a tenure-track appointment, and these academic qualifica-tions may be found in individuals other than faculty.

In community colleges, as in four-year institutions, capturing these skills most certainly requires a team approach to the development, implementation, and sustenance of any assessment of student learning effort. Ideally, a permanent core team comprised of selected faculty; deans; director of institutional assessment, research and planning; placement assessment specialist (if available); and staff from student services is needed to provide guidance and support for the institutional assessment at various levels. To the extent that the college has a faculty training center, this team would need to work closely with the staff conducting faculty training to develop adequate, ongoing training materials and approaches.

Cost of Assessment

At the time this volume is being written, public higher education across the country is facing severe budget cuts and significant increases in tuition and fees. One could argue that this is just one of many cyclical downward spirals in state funding that public higher education has been through before. However, the fiscal reality of many community colleges—in good and, more so, in bad times—poses serious questions regarding the institutional capacity for conducting meaningful, long-term, and sustained assessment.

The cost of conducting assessment of student learning has received relatively little attention and analysis. Lewis (1988) noted the lack of information in this area as early as 1988 and little has changed since. However, it is fairly common in community colleges that 80 percent or more of operational budgets is tied to salary and benefits; most of the remainder is tied to fixed costs. Discretionary money to fund assessment efforts is scarce.

For colleges that have not created an infrastructure capable of sustaining assessment of student learning outcomes, re-allocation of existing resources may be the best avenue to begin engagement in such a process. Grants can also facilitate focused assessment efforts. However, assessment frameworks built on grants may not be sustained over time without institutional commitment of resources. Some states have adopted performance funding mechanisms as a way to promote accountability tied directly to financial rewards (Burke and Serban, 1998). Institutions beginning to engage in assessment or trying to re-shape their existing practices should give careful consideration not only to the processes and uses of assessment, but also to the direct and indirect costs of conducting assessment and their implications for faculty and staff workload and administrative overhead.

Conclusion

This chapter focused on institutional assessment of student learning outcomes in community colleges, the skills needed to conduct effective assessment, and associated cost considerations. Missing from literature in the field are comprehensive models that would guide community colleges in developing an assessment approach that coherently integrates all levels, from courses and programs to the overall institution. Such models should specify the student learning outcomes to be assessed, related assessment tools and techniques, relevant methods for collecting and analyzing data, and strategies for linking the results of assessment to overall planning and evaluation processes in order to improve outcomes. Accrediting agencies should work closely with college practitioners, researchers, assessment specialists, and other agencies to develop integrated models for identifying, assessing, measuring, and applying student learning outcomes in a comprehensive manner that is within the capacity of community colleges to implement and sustain.

References

Anandam, K. "A New Direction for Developmental Education Using Technology." Paper presented at the Annual Convention of the American Association of Community Colleges, Washington, D.C., April 1994. (ED 368 420)

Astin, A. W. *Assessment for Excellence.* Phoenix: Oryx Press, 1993.

Bers, T. H., Davis, B. D., and Taylor, B. "The Use of Syllabi in Assessments: Unobtrusive Indicators and Tools for Faculty Development." *Assessment Update,* 2000, 12(3), 4–7.

Burke, J. C., and Serban, A. M. (eds.). *Performance Funding for Public Higher Education: Fad or Trend?* New Directions for Institutional Research, no. 97. San Francisco: Jossey-Bass, 1998.

Davis, B. G. "Demystifying Assessment: Learning from the Field of Evaluation." In P. J. Gray (ed.), *Achieving Assessment Goals Using Evaluation Techniques.* New Directions for Higher Education, no. 67. San Francisco: Jossey Bass, 1989.

Ewell, P. T. "Some Implications for Practice." In P. T. Ewell (ed.), *Assessing Educational Outcomes.* New Directions for Institutional Research, no. 47. San Francisco: Jossey-Bass, 1985.

Ewell, P. T. "Establishing a Campus-Based Assessment Program." In D. F. Halpern (ed.), *Student Outcomes Assessment: What Institutions Stand to Gain.* New Directions for Higher Education, no. 59. San Francisco: Jossey-Bass, 1987.

Keup, J. R. "Using Technology in Remedial Education." *ERIC Digest,* 1998. (ED 421 180)

Lewis, D. R. "Costs and Benefits of Assessment: A Paradigm." In T. W. Banta (ed.), *Implementing Outcomes Assessment: Promise and Perils.* New Directions for Institutional Research, no. 59. San Francisco: Jossey-Bass, 1988.

Moore, A. "Computer Assisted Instruction (ILS) for Adults." Paper presented at the Annual International Conference of the National Institute for the Staff and Organizational Development on Teaching Excellence and Conference Administrators, Austin, Tex., May 1993. (ED 377 897)

National Center for Education Statistics. Remedial Education at Higher Education Institutions in Fall 2000. Washington, D.C.: U.S. Department of Education, 2003.

Palomba, C. A., and Banta, T. W. *Assessment Essentials: Planning, Implementing, and Improving Assessment in Higher Education.* San Francisco: Jossey-Bass, 1999.

Robertson, S. N., and Simpson, C. A. "General Education Discipline Evaluation Process for the Community College." In T. W. Banta, J. P. Lund, K. E. Black, and F. W. Oblander (eds.), *Assessment in Practice: Putting Principles to Work on College Campuses.* San Francisco: Jossey-Bass, 1996.

Volkwein, J. F. "Implementing Outcomes Assessment on Your Campus." The RP Group *eJournal*, 1, May 2003. http://rpgroup.org/publications/eJournal/Volume_1/volume_1.htm. Accessed February 16, 2004.

Wilson, A. M. "The INVEST Program: A Computer-Based System for Adult Academic Upgrading. A Pilot Study." Research report, Cumberland Campus of Nova Scotia Community College, 1992. (ED 377 896)

Yamasaki, E. "Effective Policies for Remedial Education." *ERIC Digest*, 1998. (ED 416 940)

ANDREEA M. SERBAN is associate vice president for information resources and director of institutional assessment, research, and planning at Santa Barbara City College in Santa Barbara, California.

3

Outcomes. Alternative assessment. Multiple measures. Analysis. Data. How does an institution move from academic discourse to authentic assessment of student learning? The answer is to engage the faculty and students in the process.

Engaging Faculty and Students in Classroom Assessment of Learning

Fay Rouseff-Baker, Andrew Holm

> There is widespread agreement that college administrators and faculty can no longer dodge, ignore, or poorly respond to questions from stakeholders about what and how well students are learning.
> J. E. Roueche, M. D. Milliron, and S. D. Roueche, 2003, p. 97.

In the late 1980s, the Higher Learning Commission of the North Central Association (Higher Learning Commission of NCA) called on all of its affiliated institutions to assess and document academic achievement. Since 1989, the administration and faculty at Parkland College (Illinois) have planned and developed systems and strategies to do so. Although a driving force at Parkland was to satisfy the accrediting agency, the more fundamental motivation was to shift the focus of the college culture to improved student education. Changing pedagogy would result only if assessment was faculty driven and resulted in critical reflection on teaching and learning. To quote Cross (1997), "The goal is to engage faculty in continuing conversations about teaching and learning and to encourage teachers to join together with teaching colleagues and students in developing a climate of inquiry about learning" (p. 18). The information gathered on student learning would then be used to improve courses in order to help more students succeed.

The purpose of this chapter is to share strategies and systems that engage community college faculty and students in the process of assessing student learning at the classroom level. Examples from Parkland College illustrate strategies to equip faculty with tools for insights and analysis so that questions from stakeholders can be addressed. Systems necessary to provide requisite support from the institution and to inspire and perpetuate the scholarship of teaching and learning are also described. The result of combining appropriate systems and strategies is a fuller participation by both faculty and students in authentic, ongoing assessment.

Classroom Assessment

Throughout the last decade, Parkland College has continued to improve its assessment process. In 1998, the college's administration invited Parkland's Center of Excellence in Teaching and Learning (the Center), an ongoing professional development system for faculty, to explore possible connections between classroom assessment and the larger assessment process. Parkland's executive vice president asked a core group of faculty who were passionate about assessment at the classroom level to link their interests with larger institutional concerns. Key faculty leaders rose to the challenge; the resulting synergy produced an effective blending of proven classroom instruments with more traditional assessment methods. Four guiding questions evolved in response to stakeholders' concerns:

- What are we doing? (goals and objectives)
- Is it working? (assessment tools)
- How do we know? (data gathering)
- What changes are we making? (adaptations)

These questions and the following Feedback Loop (Figure 3.1) frame the discussion of assessment that follows.

Since 1996, the Center has offered classroom assessment courses to faculty every semester; more than three hundred faculty have voluntarily taken these courses. These courses model the Feedback Loop, which is at the heart of the assessment process. It is the completion of the Feedback Loop that leads to positive change for students in the classroom.

Classroom Assessment Techniques (CATs)

Angelo and Cross (1993) describe a system for assessing classroom work. Through research involving hundreds of faculty nationwide, they developed the concept of Classroom Assessment and Research. Angelo de-scribes classroom assessment as the systematic and on-going study of what and how students are learning in a particular classroom. The tools applied in this systematic study are Classroom Assessment Techniques (CATs). They are quick, simple, and usually anonymous tools that help to gather feedback from students on their learning. At Parkland College, faculty use CATs to investigate learning issues; they then share their results with other faculty in written reports and oral presentations.

Figure 3.1. The Classroom Assessment Process

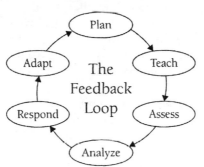

The following example illustrates a cohesive framework for course-level assessment where CATs complement traditional assessment tools. A group of six full-time faculty and four part-time faculty who teach Psychology 101 met and, after much discussion, came to agreement on the course content goals they would assess. The group then devised a set of assessment questions—multiple-choice and application—aligned with these goals. All faculty administered the questions by embedding them into their final exams. The data were broken out, giving the professors their individual results along with the collective results at the course level. The information was used to reevaluate the quality of the questions and the learning goals.

The following semester, one of the professors began her 200-level psychology class by issuing a CAT. She asked the students to respond anonymously to the same assessment questions given at the end of Psychology 101. The CAT results helped her to assess the background knowledge her students brought with them from 100-level courses. In addition, the discussion that took place while completing the Feedback Loop was enlightening. The students became more connected to the notion that they were to learn important content and apply that content. Subsequently, the professor made adaptations to her teaching strategies by revising test questions and allocating more time to certain content and to writing assignments. She then took the results from this CAT and others used throughout the semester back to her psychology colleagues, completing the Feedback Loop at the collective course level. Further adaptations were then made at the course and classroom level from information gathered through the application of these complementary models of assessment.

Student Engagement

Traditional assessment tools often bypass the students when it comes to processing and using the results. With CATs, students are invited to be part of gathering, assessing, analyzing, and acting upon the evidence that they provide. When students complete a CAT and hear about the results from their instructor, they are involved in the process of metacognition: thinking about thinking and learning. Together, faculty and students can then consider ways to adapt and improve the instructional process. Students realize that faculty care about their learning and value their participation in the learning process. Indeed, the success of any assessment process depends on continued and honest participation from the students involved. A shift occurs when the students become valued participants; a powerful dynamic emerges between the teacher and the taught. In addition, Fabry, Eisenbach, and Gordon (1997) found that students exposed to CATs reported improved understanding of course material and had a more favorable attitude toward instruction. The process of using CATs produces valuable information that supplies a basis for rich and meaningful discussion between students and the teacher, which can lead to important course improvements.

For example, a veterinary technology instructor at Parkland used the Memory Matrix, a CAT designed to improve recall of information (Angelo and Cross, 1993). This CAT resembled a quiz: students were asked to categorize common veterinary drugs, describing how they worked, the type of pain treated, and the possible side effects. After reviewing students' work, the instructor gave feedback to the students, clarifying misconceptions and giving suggestions to prepare for the next quiz. The result was the highest quiz average in the five years that the class had been taught. More important, 50 percent of the students changed their study techniques based on the instructor's advice. Using a similar CAT six weeks after the material was covered, the instructor found students' ability to categorize drugs and their long-term memory of the terms had improved in 80 percent of the drug categories. Student feedback indicated that they had improved their review strategies and were continuing to try new techniques for study and review. This example clearly supports the importance of student engagement in the assessment process.

Faculty Engagement

Although accrediting bodies make it clear that the preferred units of measure for academic assessment are the larger units such as course clusters, programs, or departments, it is also very important to tie assessment of learning outcomes to the classroom. As Diaz-Lefebvre (2003) asserts: "An important characteristic of an effective assessment program is that it be faculty owned and driven. Whatever measure is used, it needs to be continually evaluated for appropriateness and fit in measuring the content and extent of student learning the faculty has intended. Institutional efforts at assessment and improvement of student learning at the educational program level ultimately depend on research, assessment, and improved learning at the classroom level" (p. 2). Since students and faculty interact most directly in classroom settings rather than in the program or department settings, it seems reasonable to use the classroom as the appropriate environment for assessment of learning outcomes. Of course, classroom-level assessment can also inform assessment efforts at the levels of program, department, or institution (Angelo, 1998). According to Lopez (1996), the research methods and assessment techniques that have worked well for an individual instructor in improving his or her teaching and increasing the learning of students in the classroom are likely to be directly applicable or adaptable to the assessment and improvement of learning at the programmatic level.

Angelo and Cross (1993) developed CATs as tools for periodic assessment of student learning at the classroom level on the assumption that the classroom was the appropriate unit of analysis. Parkland faculty offer positive reviews after using CATs for academic assessment. In an informal survey, one instructor noted, "faculty ownership improves the odds that assessment will be meaningful and lasting." Another observed, "CATs can give me information on results of academic assessment so that an improvement plan would be more effective. CATs could give me information relating to the validity of assessment measures." A third faculty member added, "I am particularly attracted to the idea that CATs connect the students to the assessment process. Making them a more integral part helps them complete an important loop: feedback. It makes the entire assessment process continuous and responsive." (Personal communications, March 2002.)

As these quotations reflect, the use of CATs help faculty become genuinely engaged and involved in the larger assessment process. As faculty experience immediate classroom improvements that result from the use of CATs, they become increasingly convinced that this is indeed a worthwhile process. As faculty ownership becomes apparent in the assessment process, faculty are motivated to remain engaged and their interest is more likely to be sustained over the years that follow, even after the accreditation self-study has come and gone. CATs can be invaluable tools that help make important links between classroom, program, department and institution-wide assessments, engaging both students and faculty along the way.

The Center has presented CAT work at twenty-four colleges and at numerous conferences. The response has been enthusiastic; many faculty see the importance of CATs in the assessment process. However, some of the faculty in attendance question the amount of time required to use them correctly. A response to such a question might be "How much time does it take to grade bad papers?" In other words, applying CATs while there is still time to make mid-course adjustments (formative assessment) results in better student learning by the end of the course (summative assessment) and saves time grading bad papers or exams. The reality is that teaching takes time and that "teaching without learning is just talking" (Cross, 1993, p. 3). Faculty who use CATs save time and energy while facilitating better student learning outcomes in the long run.

Examples of Outcomes Assessed by CATs

CATs take a variety of forms depending on what outcomes are being assessed. For example, an instructor of linear algebra at Parkland College sought to measure student understanding of concepts and theories using a Directed Paraphrasing CAT. "In this CAT, students are directed to paraphrase part of a lesson for a specific audience and purpose, using their own words" (Angelo and Cross, 1993, p. 232). As a complement to an exam measuring computational skills, the CAT revealed that the students lacked the ability to paraphrase the key idea of the unit. As a result, this instructor increased the time spent on difficult topics and incorporated more illustrative examples. Results on the next exam showed improved computational skills on more than half of the targeted skills in addition to an increased understanding of the process of problem solving.

An introductory psychology instructor sought to measure student understanding of concepts and theories by using the Muddiest Point CAT. "This certain CAT asks students to jot down one point that was not clear–or [is] still 'muddy'" (Angelo and Cross, 1993, p. 154). With this CAT, the instructor identified two key areas students had not mastered from a lesson on motivation theory and eating disorders. After gathering additional feedback, he altered his instruction by using more group activities, changing his review procedures, and altering his instructional handouts. The follow-up quiz showed an increased understanding of the two areas of concern. Similarly, another instructor of writing skills sought to identify students' patterns in writing development using a Background Knowledge Probe CAT. "This CAT is designed to collect much more specific, and more useful, feedback on students' prior learning" (Angelo and Cross, 1993, p. 121). The CAT helped this instructor to identify and address specific weaknesses in students' writing before the summative assessment on those writing skills. The students' next writing assignment showed an improvement in two out of the three weak areas.

In another example, an instructor of horticulture sought to assess students' understanding of key terms and facts in agriculture by using the Empty Outlines CAT. "The instructor provides students with an empty or partially completed outline of an in-class presentation or homework assignment and gives them a limited amount of time to fill in the blank spaces" (Angelo and Cross, 1993, p. 138). Through this CAT, the horticulture instructor identified concepts that students missed while viewing a video and was able to address those areas with a modified lecture and discussion format. Anecdotal evidence pointed to an increased understanding of the previously misunderstood concepts.

Value of Assessment Courses for Faculty

An important goal of academic assessment is instructional change to promote student learning. Cohen (1980) observes that "augmented" feedback, which includes consultation with someone knowledgeable in instructional processes, results in instructors receiving higher end-of-term global ratings from students than those instructors who do not discuss their results with a knowledgeable person.

Classroom Assessment and Research courses are forums for discussion of ongoing classroom investigations. Informed by the appropriate literature, faculty reflect on issues related to assessment of student learning and results of instructional improvement. Student feedback collected by the use of CATs is central to this entire process. This shift to a climate of inquiry about learning helps to answer the questions raised by stakeholders about student learning in the classroom.

Ewell (1998a) states that the strategy used to engage people in conversation is more important than the instrument used. Such a conversation among Parkland faculty has grown out of discussions about CATs and other assessment tools. For example, sharing program assessment results in developmental courses has stimulated an extensive conversation about the scientific method among faculty in the natural sciences department. As a result, presentation of the scientific method has become more consistent across disciplines and there is greater consistency in the terminology used in labs. Students are less confused and can work with the scientific method more effectively in designing and implementing lab projects.

Many Parkland faculty who have learned about CATs in the Classroom Assessment and Research courses have remained actively involved in ongoing classroom assessment since they completed the courses. Classroom Assessment courses meet eight times throughout the year and use the Parkland College *Introduction to Classroom Assessment and Research Notebook* and the Angelo and Cross text as the main resources. Several faculty who have been frustrated, disinterested, or reluctant to become involved in academic assessment have been drawn into the process through CATs. Over the last eight years, the faculty have produced more than four hundred reports on classroom assessment that provide clear evidence of honest classroom investigation into student learning. These reports serve as artifacts to be viewed by external agencies, stakeholders, and other faculty looking for improvement in student learning outcomes. Classroom Assessment courses seem to generate some of the desired outcomes for genuine institutional change that accrediting agencies are seeking.

Various institutional components play complementary roles in Parkland's ongoing academic assessment. The Academic Assessment Committee and the General Education Committee are faculty-led committees that prove very effective in launching and perpetuating assessment work at department, program, and course levels. Yet it is the system driven by the Center that enables and supports faculty to continue at the classroom level. Due to the hundreds of faculty who have enrolled in the Center's assessment courses, many faculty are familiar with CATs and the Feedback Loop and understand that student learning is central to the mission of the college. Faculty are engaged in assessing their students' learning while actively engaging in their own learning.

Using CATs to Link Classroom and Program Assessment

The Hospitality Program provides one example of how the implementation of CATs has linked classroom and program assessment. In spring 1998, an instructor in the Hospitality Program became interested in whether students underperformed in the classroom because they lacked confidence in their abilities. He developed a Self-Confidence CAT and worked with it over the next few semesters, continuously revising and improving it. As a result of using this CAT, the instructor adjusted his approach to counseling the students about their future careers. He encouraged students to make appointments with him earlier in the semester to talk about their grades, their feelings, and their careers. His role in the classroom shifted from the omniscient expert to a caring, approachable teacher. An important shift in the instructional dynamic between this teacher and his students is evident from the increased interaction between them both inside and outside the classroom.

This instructor's Self-Confidence CAT eventually became part of the overall program assessment due to its proven impact on the classroom. The CAT served as a tool to complement other program assessment methods because it addressed this confidence issue, which was important to the overall program assessment but had not been previously addressed. This example illustrates that blending classroom and program assessment helps faculty obtain a fuller picture of both. For this instructor, CATs provided an entry point to deeper and broader engagement in assessment of student learning outcomes.

Community college ESL courses and programs offer additional opportunities for use of CATs. Often students in these classes are coming from extreme conditions of deprivation and have had limited access to paper, not to mention computers. Furthermore, many students come from cultures with oral traditions where academic systems often put a high value on student recitation and less value on written forms. Therefore, even students with fairly functional language skills may lack the most basic academic literacy skills, including how to interact with the instructor, respond to due dates, ask questions about assignment requirements, and produce an acceptable academic product.

In addition to teaching and measuring basic literacy skills, one of the goals across the Parkland College Intensive ESL program is to teach students about American culture. Students from other types of educational systems often do not understand how independent and self-reliant college students are expected to be in the United States, and this lack of understanding may impede learning.

An ESL Instructor at Parkland College applies CATs at both the classroom and program level. The CAT in Exhibit 3.1 is given in eleven ESL sections twice each year, once just before midterm and once in the last week

Exhibit 3.1. ESL Student Satisfaction and Responsibility CAT

Class: _____   Instructor: _____

Rate these statements:	Very true				Not true
I go to class everyday.	1	2	3	4	5
I work hard on homework assignments.	1	2	3	4	5
I ask questions in class.	1	2	3	4	5
I often study with friends.	1	2	3	4	5
I am using the language lab for extra practice.	1	2	3	4	5
I enjoy coming to class.	1	2	3	4	5
I think my English is improving.	1	2	3	4	5

of classes. The results of the CATs are analyzed by each instructor, shared with the students, and brought back to the collective ESL faculty. After comparing the results they receive, faculty adapt their teaching strategies and course content.

This CAT doubles as an assessment tool for program satisfaction and helps raise student awareness of their role in the education process. The information from this assessment tool can help students see that a strong relationship exists between participating in their learning and ultimately being successful in the program.

Another example comes from the Surgical Technology Program at Parkland College, in which students did not achieve program goals in four surgical task areas. These problem areas were identified through the use of direct and indirect learning outcomes, and a diagnostic CAT was used to determine what changes should be made in the pre-clinical training. The CAT identified the student-to-faculty ratio as one area needing to be improved. The faculty proposed and made changes in the ratio and will again assess to determine effectiveness. In this case, the CAT did not assess learning outcomes, but helped diagnose how well the learning environment affected the student learning process and gave the administration necessary information for decision making.

Assessing both Process and Outcomes

During a 1999 consultation at Parkland College, Ewell emphasized the importance of gathering input on "enabling conditions," so that if satisfactory outcomes are not achieved, faculty have some information on what took place during the process of instruction. According to Ewell, "We should not just focus on outcomes, but we should be asking how the curriculum works (focus on the stimulus end, not just the responses)" (P. T. Ewell, personal consultation, March 25, 1999). Understanding the balance between the instructional process (stimulus) and the learning outcomes (response) of a learning experience is essential to effective assessment and could even be written into college assessment plans as part of the popular focus on learning outcomes.

The following quotation further illuminates the balance between process and learning outcomes assessment:

> The current format for reporting program assessment is excellent because it focuses attention on the need to establish and document concrete learning outcomes. But programs should also be encouraged to establish objectives focused on the learning processes needed to attain these outcomes—for example, specific curricular features or pedagogies that they want to engage in. In short, all programs must establish and communicate learning outcomes through the reporting format, but they certainly should not be prohibited from also communicating plans for examining curricular features and processes. Doing so might provide some faculties with more concreteness in the process, as well as providing a link to program review [P. T. Ewell, personal consultation, March 25, 1999].

In most assessment, the emphasis is clearly on well-stated objectives that focus on outcomes assessment. In fact, the Higher Learning Commission of NCA adopted student outcomes assessment as one of its requirements in 1989. However, many faculty find that there is an important interplay between process and outcomes assessment. Diaz-Lefebvre (2003) emphasizes that it is important to focus not only on outcomes but also on the experiences that lead up to those outcomes. Heady, Coppola, and Titterington (2001) echo that emphasis and stress that one way to get at process is to periodically sample the materials used along the way. By doing so, the classroom becomes an ongoing series of snapshots of learning issues—both students and faculty are increasingly engaged in the conversation that emerges. The focus shifts from simply assessing product to also assessing the pathway that led to that product.

Angelo and Cross (1993) developed CATs as tools for formative assessment—to assess instruction while it is in progress rather than after it has been completed. An example of this type of assessment comes from the Natural Sciences department at Parkland College. Since spring 1998, instructors in Chemistry 101 have used course-embedded assessment on the second hour-long exam to assess problem-solving skills on several important concepts. Data have been collected each fall using item analysis so that they could be reviewed to see how well students were succeeding on those particular problem-solving skills.

In fall 2000, five different instructors collected data in a "course cluster" of six sections of Chemistry 101. As the instructors looked at the Preliminary data, they noticed that many of the students did worse on the second exam in comparison to the first. Instructors initially assumed that they had not taught the material relating to the second exam as well and began to discuss ways to alter and improve their teaching. However, it soon occurred to them to test their assumptions first. They decided to give a CAT to all six sections to find out more about student perceptions of the exam. The CAT was completed by 94 of the 112 students (84 percent) who took the exam. Sixty-seven percent of those students indicated that they had done worse on the second exam compared to the first exam. Why did they do worse? Half of the students thought the material was more difficult; one-quarter studied less; half had more complicated lives; one-quarter worked more hours; and one-quarter had worse health.

The five instructors met to look at these data and other item analyses. After a lengthy discussion, the coordinator of Chemistry 101 decided to give a Faculty CAT to the instructors to gather some anonymous feedback on the "enabling conditions" in the classroom. Was there sufficient opportunity to learn the material? Was there an appropriate environment for learning the material? Based on the results of the feedback from both the students and the faculty, a number of decisions were made, including discontinuing the use of electronic quizzes until frustrating technical difficulties were corrected; gathering input from all participating instructors in writing the common course quizzes; rewriting some course objectives and exam questions to clarify their wording; looking for additional CD-ROM and video resources to supplement the material; discussing with students their workload and other outside pressures; and trying new strategies and incentives to inspire students to complete more homework. Instructional change was certainly the result of this process as well as changes in the following types of outcomes:

Reduced student confusion and complaints about fairness and wording on quizzes and exams as a result of clarifying objectives and joint authorship

More discussion with students on appropriate ratios of work load to course load, leading to more sensible schedules

Increased completion of homework assignments as a result of greater emphasis and periodic sampling as part of students' participation grade

General improvement in retention (an average of 68 percent in the four semesters before 2000 and an average of 74 percent in the four most recent semesters)

Importance of Using Multiple Measures

Effective assessment of complex student learning relies on gathering multiple measures or indicators of learning from a variety of sources. Examples of commonly used multiple measures are standardized tests, course-embedded questions on common exams, performance assessments, surveys of student and faculty attitudes, pretesting and posttesting, periodic sampling of writing and computational skills, and portfolios. These may be categorized as either direct or indirect measures. Direct measures assess the knowledge and skills students have learned by having them actually demonstrate their learning by writing, doing calculations, and problem solving. Indirect measures gather opinions from students and employees about their learning.

One type of direct measure is performance assessment, where students are asked to accomplish multiple steps in a problem-solving sequence. In science courses, for example, performance assessment can be useful in laboratories to see if students understand which equipment to use, how to use it for various purposes, and what to do with the data they compile. This type of assessment engages and motivates students more extensively than traditional assessment methods. According to Ewell (1998b), the trend toward the use of these more authentic and real-world assessments is one of the "three broad trends now observable in the ongoing practice of assessment at the institutional level" (p. 110).

For example, in the Chemistry 101 courses at Parkland College, the same performance assessment on the property of density was administered in all sections over several fall semesters. After doing a lab on density, each student was given a solution of unknown density. Students then had to choose the right equipment, make all necessary measurements, record the correct data, and finally, calculate the density of the unknown solution. As the faculty looked at the data, an important ongoing conversation developed among the chemistry staff that generated the following analysis and actions:

A series of general lab objectives was developed in cognitive, affective, and psychomotor domains. These objectives were used as a template for the organization of chemistry labs and for assessment of the knowledge, attitudes, and skills needed to succeed in such labs.

Assessment and instruction were intertwined in such a way as to teach lab skills more effectively. Students would now be assessed, evaluated, retaught, and reassessed until skills improve to an acceptable level.

A specific scoring rubric was developed for each step in the performance assessment and given to students before the assessment took place. As a result, students better understand what is expected of them and instructors will have a more consistent way of grading their work.

Data collected so far have shown an improvement in the proper use of lab procedures and lab equipment as well as a higher percentage of correct calculations of density.

CATs and Improved Student Learning

In fall 2003, a social science professor completed an analysis of a sampling of final reports from faculty participants in the Center's introductory course on college assessment. In her analysis, the professor looked for evidence of significant changes in teaching and for the perception of notable improvements in student learning. In the seventy-eight reports examined, one hundred and fifty comments reported clear and strong evidence of changes as a result of participation in the course. In fact, every faculty member reported at least one significant change in teaching; most reported at least two.

In sixty-one of the seventy-eight reports, faculty said they saw clear improvements in students' learning. Those improvements were in the areas of increased active learning (27 percent), improved metacognition (22 percent), improved positive affect toward learning (22 percent), enhanced academic confidence (11 percent), acquisition of new knowledge (10 percent), and development of new skills (9 percent). Her conclusion was that, after participating in the courses, these seventy-eight faculty improved their ability to reach and teach their students, becoming more learner-centered. It was evident to these faculty members that by listening to students through feedback and responding to their concerns, they were better able to address important learning issues that emerged and see positive changes in student behavior.

Conclusion

The importance of fully engaging faculty and students in the assessment process cannot be overemphasized. If a college wants a systematic, sustainable process, efforts must be made to draw participants into the process in a meaningful way. Classroom Assessment Techniques are tools that allow faculty to investigate students' learning and to make appropriate adjustments for student success. As a result, faculty are invigorated, students are engaged, and the institutional culture is energized.

Finally, it is the dynamic engagement of administration, faculty, and students that makes the assessment process authentic. The strategies described in this chapter are based on the work of hundreds of faculty who have risen to the challenge of answering the question: "What and how well are students learning?"

References

American Association of Higher Education. "Principles of Good Practice for Assessing Student Learning." http://www.ualr.edu/~provost/assessdocs/AAHEprin.html. Accessed Feb. 24, 2004.

Angelo, T. A. Assessment Institute in Indianapolis. Indiana University–Purdue University Indianapolis. Nov. 8–11, 1998.

Angelo, T. A., and Cross, K. P. *Classroom Assessment Techniques: A Handbook for College Teachers.* (2nd ed.) San Francisco: Jossey-Bass, 1993.

Cohen, P. A. "Effectiveness of Student-Rating Feedback for Improving College Instruction: A Meta-Analysis of Findings." *Research in Higher Education,* 1980, 13(4).

Cross, K. P. "Developing Professional Fitness Through Classroom Assessment and Classroom Research." *The Cross Papers, 1,* Sept. 1997.

Diaz-Lefebvre, R. "In the Trenches: Assessment as if Understanding Mattered." 2003. http://www.league.org/publication/abstracts/learning/lelabs0308.htm. Accessed Feb. 24, 2004.

Ewell, P. T. Assessment Institute in Indianapolis. Indiana University–Purdue University Indianapolis. Nov. 8–11, 1998a.

Ewell, P. T. "National Trends in Assessing Student Learning." *Journal of Engineering Education,* 1998b, 87(2), 107–113.

Fabry, V., Eisenbach, R., and Gordon, V. L. "Thanks for Asking: Classroom Assessment Techniques and Students' Perceptions of Learning." *Journal on Excellence in College Teaching*, 1997, 8(1), 3–21.

Heady, J. E., Coppola, B. P., and Titterington, L. C. *"Assessment Standards. College Pathways to the Science Education Standards."* Arlington, Va.: National Science Teachers Association Press, 2001.

Holm, A., and Rouseff-Baker, F. *Introduction to Classroom Assessment and Research Notebook.* (16th ed.) Champaign, Ill.: Parkland College, 2002.

Lopez, C. *Opportunities for Improvement: Advice from Consultant-Evaluators on Programs to Assess Student Learning.* Chicago: North Central Accreditation Commission on Institutions of Higher Education, March 1996, 13–15.

Parkland College. "Academic Assessment." http://www.parkland.edu/aac/overview.htm. Accessed Jan. 11, 2004.

Roueche, J. E., Milliron, M. D., and Roueche, S. D. *Practical Magic: On the Front Lines of Teaching Excellence.* Washington, D.C.: Community College Press, 2003.

FAY ROUSEFF-BAKER is executive director of the Center for Excellence in Teaching and Learning and associate professor of English at Parkland College, Champaign, Illinois.

ANDREW HOLM is professor of chemistry and coordinator of classroom assessment at Parkland College, Champaign, Illinois.

4

Program-level assessments at community colleges are particularly challenging because students often achieve their goals without completing a program, or they select an array of courses that suit their needs but do not fit within an officially recognized program of study.

Assessment at the Program Level

Trudy H. Bers

Program-level assessment is a particularly challenging task in community colleges, yet one that accrediting agencies, many state governing or coordinating boards, and the public expect colleges to perform. The purpose of this chapter is to address issues of program-level assessment, with an emphasis on programs that do not have to meet external accreditation criteria, vendor or professional licensure or certification examinations, or generally accepted skill hierarchies, such as those that exist in mathematics or composition.

According to Palomba and Banta (1999), programmatic assessment "helps determine whether students can integrate learning from individual courses into a coherent whole. It is interested in the cumulative effects of the educational process" (p. 5–6). Program-level assessment may focus on the extent to which each student in a program acquires the knowledge, skills, beliefs, and feelings specified as program outcomes. Program-level assessment may also focus on gauging the learning of a group of students in the program, rather than each student within it. When assessment concentrates on individual students, feedback provides them with important information about the extent to which they have met program learning objectives. When assessment concentrates on a group of students in a program, outcomes information is of more value to the department or institution, as it can be used to improve courses, programs, and services.

In community colleges, program-level assessment is easiest for programs with external accreditation requirements driving the curriculum and compelling students to complete the program before they can enter the field or take licensure or certifying examinations, and programs that prepare students for vendor or industry certification examinations. Many programs in the health careers and selected technologies (such as Microsoft Certified Systems Engineer and Certified Novell Engineer) fit this model. Program-level assessment is far more challenging in other programs for a host of reasons described below.

What Is a Program?

This seems like a simple, almost nonsensical, question. However, the definition of a "program" at community colleges is neither clear nor consistent. The multiplicity of activities referred to as programs have implications for the assessment of student learning outcomes as well. A program may consist of any of the following groups of courses:

A Sequence of Prescribed Courses. Nursing is an example of a program that is based on a structured sequence of courses that may or may not include general-education courses or electives and that leads to an officially recognized associate degree or certificate upon completion of courses and meeting other college graduation requirements. Other programs of this type include community college marketing or management programs, which will probably have more variety in courses than will a nursing program. In addition, students enrolled in marketing or management programs may be less interested in earning a degree because the associate degree is not typically a required credential to work in these fields.

The General Education Component of an Associate Degree. General education is most often defined as a distribution of courses in liberal arts and sciences, though some schools permit selected vocational courses to satisfy general education requirements. In community colleges, general education is often administered through departments such as English and social science rather than through a department or division of general education. Accrediting agencies such as the Higher Learning Commission of the North Central Association expect community colleges to assess student learning outcomes in general education, and sometimes institutions refer to their "general education programs." Chapter Eight further addresses assessment of student outcomes in general education.

Courses in a Specific Discipline. This use of the term "program" overlaps with its use in referring to freshman–sophomore courses a student should take if he or she is planning to major in and earn a bachelor's degree in the field, such as mathematics or psychology. What, however, is a community college's "mathematics program" or "psychology program"?

Among the challenges associated with assessing this type of program is identifying students who have taken the courses the college specifies as part of the program. Because community college students frequently depart from an institution or step out for one or more semesters before completing a predetermined set of courses, it is difficult to target many who have taken most of a set of courses and will be available for assessment activities. Thus assessment for these types of programs must often rely on college records such as transcripts, or on student work completed in courses, or practicums considered to be capstone or end-of-program learning experiences.

Precollegiate or Remedial Courses. Many institutions offer "remedial programs," particularly in English and mathematics. These may be housed within a single remedial education department or may be decentralized to the disciplines. They may be administered through academic or through student affairs areas, taught by faculty whose appointment is in the remedial program or by faculty in the disciplines who teach one or more remedial courses as part of their regular workloads. They may count toward financial aid or not, or accrue credits applicable to a particular degree or not. Moreover, a remedial program might include a cohort of students barred from taking other courses until they meet college-level skills requirements of the institution, or it may include all students taking a remedial course even if they enroll simultaneously in college-level courses. Clearly, then, remedial programs reflect a wide variety of alternatives in terms of administration, instruction, and their place in the college's academic offerings.

Assessing student learning outcomes in remedial programs is relatively easy when programs consist of sequences of remedial courses leading to entry into college-level courses, especially when placement tests are used for course entry and exit decisions, course content is skill-based (as is the case in mathematics and composition), and remedial students are restricted from taking college-level courses. Assessment is more challenging when placement is advisory rather than prescriptive, when students take remedial courses voluntarily, or when students take college-level courses simultaneously.

Special Programs for Selected Students. These programs include students who meet eligibility requirements or volunteer to be involved and who may be engaged in honors programs, TRIO programs, service learning programs, Perkins programs, and first-year-in-college programs. Students may take certain courses, receive support services, engage in specific activities, or simply meet threshold criteria to be included. Sometimes program involvement is invisible for the student; how many students identify themselves as "Perkins students," for example?

Some special programs already rely on performance indicators to assess student outcomes. In Illinois, for example, the Perkins programs use measures such as percentage of students who graduate, or percentage who obtain and retain employment as indicators of program effectiveness and, indirectly if not directly, as indicators of student learning. Studies of students engaged in service learning are beginning to appear; certainly many institutions ask students involved in service learning projects whether and what they believe they have learned from these experiences. Special programs vary tremendously with respect to reporting requirements, ability with which program staff can and do identify and track students associated with the program, and extent to which program students comprise a discrete group or blend into the regular college population.

It is clear from the array of programs described above that the term program is used loosely at community colleges. Moreover, the same student may well fit within several programs, further complicating the assessment of program-level learning outcomes. Did the student achieve these outcomes from the program under scrutiny alone, or from the interaction of experiences in several college programs? Which programs should be credited (or blamed) for the outcomes?

Assessment Approaches

Many approaches are available for assessing student outcomes at the program level, though some are more feasible than others.

Capstone Courses. Some programs have a capstone course, a required class at the end of the program that integrates material covered earlier and allows students to demonstrate their learning through various combinations of tests, papers, portfolios, simulations, team assignments, presentations, and other methods for demonstrating learning. The instructor of record, several faculty members in the program, an advisory committee or other industry practitioners, or a combination of these can evaluate student learning in capstone courses. Although with Capstone Courses assessment is technically occurring at the course level, the courses are designed to approximate the totality of key learning expected of students completing a program. Therefore course learning outcomes can also be interpreted as program-level learning outcomes.

Vendor or Industry Certification Examination. Some fields, especially those in technology, are experiencing a growth of certification examinations administered by vendors or professional and industry organizations. Certification is external validation that the student has acquired knowledge and skills identified by the vendor or organization as essential for a particular job or credential. The examining body may not care where test takers obtained their knowledge, and they may not even care whether this was achieved through coursework or self-study. Community colleges may develop programs intended to prepare students for these examinations, however, and use results as indicators of program-level learning.

Institutional or Departmental Testing. This approach requires faculty to agree on one or more standardized or institutionally developed tests that cover all or most essential elements of a program. Tests are administered to all students at the completion of the program, for example at the end of a culminating course, prior to receiving a degree or certificate, or as a prerequisite for enrollment in a capstone course, practicum, or seminar experience. Because students would take the test regardless of instructor and at or near the end of the curriculum, results may be interpreted as indicating acquisition of knowledge, skills, and attitudes at the program level. However, where information about students' knowledge, skills, and attitudes at program entry are not known, such interpretations must be made with great caution. Where standardized tests are available, the testing agency will have information about validity, reliability, and norm-referenced or criterion-referenced results for prior test takers. Where departments create their own tests, evaluating test reliability and validity may be a daunting project; faculty frequently rely on face validity and assume their professional judgment is sufficient to give the test credibility.

In reality, however, both institutionally developed and standardized tests are often difficult to use in community colleges. They are not available in all areas, and it is often expensive to both create high-quality institutional tests and administer them under rigorous testing protocols. As noted in Chapter One, tests are often controversial, especially when faculty believe a standardized test does not align with program objectives. Unless test results directly affect graduation or grade-point averages, students have little incentive to take them seriously.

Satisfaction Surveys. Student and alumni satisfaction surveys that include self-reported estimates of learning provide indirect evidence of student learning outcomes. Though most powerful when results are triangulated with more direct assessments of learning, satisfaction surveys can be especially helpful when respondents are currently working in the field and are providing feedback about whether what they believe they learned in the program has adequately prepared them for the workplace. Satisfaction surveys are available through a number of commercial providers and may be institutionally developed as well.

Portfolio Assessment. Portfolios are collections of students' work that demonstrate learning and development. Work is carefully assessed by faculty or other content-area experts and typically evaluated holistically. Portfolios can consist of hard or electronic copies of students' work, or both, and may include artifacts such as student-written papers, projects, videotapes of presentations, resumes, sample letters of application for jobs, and other materials that give evidence of achievements. For program-level assessment, portfolios must contain documentation of learning and development across the spectrum of program objectives.

Performance Manuals. A performance manual lists and briefly describes behaviors a student should be able to execute with competency at the conclusion of a program. Faculty evaluate students' abilities to perform these behaviors, which may be observed in class, at clinical settings, through service learning, in other service or support activities, or elsewhere (Boland and Laidig, 2001).

Narratives. Benner (1999) suggests a novel approach to assessment: having students recount their experiences through stories while faculty assess learning by listening to and questioning students to determine whether they demonstrate understanding of the context and content of the situations they describe. This approach requires students and faculty to engage in dialogue. However, while this method may provide rich insights into how and what each student has learned, translating information into summary form for program improvement may be challenging.

Culminating Project. A culminating project may be linked with a capstone course or internship experience or it may stand alone as a requirement for program completion. The project needs to be broadly defined and reflect student learning and ability to integrate information from across the curriculum. Projects may be graded by faculty, by outside experts, or by a combination of internal and external evaluators. The project differs from a portfolio in that a portfolio is a collection of student work gathered throughout the student's time at the institution, whereas the project is a more focused work that addresses a particular situation or simulation. For example, students in fashion merchandising might be required to put together a marketing campaign including sample ads, budgets, media schedules, and displays to promote a new line of sportswear targeted to young teens, and then to present the campaign to an audience of faculty, peers, and industry representatives. In the performing arts, a "juried performance" is often used to showcase student work evaluated by outside experts.

Transfer to and Success in Another Institution. The primary purpose of community college transfer programs is to provide students with the first two years of undergraduate work and to give them the necessary knowledge and skills to succeed in upper-division coursework. Thus, an indirect indicator of student learning is acceptance at and transfer to a four-year college or university. Community colleges can find out if and where many of their students transfer through the National Student Clearinghouse Enrollment Search program. The Clearinghouse claims to have data for some 91 percent of all students enrolled in postsecondary education in the United States (National Student Clearinghouse, 2004).

Implementation Challenges

Even after conceptual and operational definitions of what constitutes a program are addressed, a second major challenge in most programs is clearly identifying students who are at the end of a program. Many students are difficult to track because they either leave a college without earning a certificate or degree, or change programs by virtue of enrolling in different courses without officially notifying the college of their changed objectives. Even when students are identified by program, it is often difficult to obtain their cooperation in taking programmatic examinations or engaging in other activities that are not specifically embedded within a course or that do not affect grade-point averages or graduation eligibility. Students rarely see a direct personal benefit in participating in program-level assessments. Even students who are willing may not have the time or flexibility to participate in an assessment activity that occurs outside their normal course schedules.

A third major challenge is to obtain faculty concurrence on what key learning outcomes should be assessed and what level of ability or knowledge students should attain to reflect adequate or excellent learning. When faculty agree in theory, they may still find it difficult to settle on specific assessment approaches or details of implementation.

A fourth major challenge is meeting resource requirements to implement some assessments. Use of commercial or standardized instruments can easily cost thousands of dollars; for example, the ACT Alumni Survey for two-year colleges, including the most basic reporting, will cost more than $600 for five hundred students, not including postage.

A fifth major challenge is sporadic or missing feedback on external certification or licensure examinations. Though community colleges may identify student success on these external measures as important indicators of student learning outcomes, the companies or agencies administering the tests may be unwilling or unable to provide information to colleges about their students' results. Schools may then need to depend on students' voluntarily reporting their results, but self-reports are prone to inaccuracy and incompleteness, and sometimes students simply do not bother to report. Issues of privacy and compliance with the Family Education Rights and Privacy Act further complicate attempts to obtain results systematically for individual students.

Another challenge is sustaining the assessment effort across multiple years. Eliciting faculty support when external incentives—especially a forthcoming accreditation visit—are strong is not always easy, but getting support when the motivation has to come from within the institution is even more difficult. Assessment may be perceived as threatening, as diverting energy from teaching, and as gathering data and information that are not fed back into the decision-making processes. While none of these views of assessment is necessarily true, the fact remains that, despite growing emphasis over the past decade on assessing learning outcomes and being more accountable for student learning, many faculty continue to question the validity of assessment and their responsibilities to assess anything other than what they do within their individual classes.

Good Practices

In preparing this chapter, I searched the literature and used a number of listservs to request examples of good practices of program-level assessments in community colleges. In keeping with the primary focus of this chapter, I emphasized examples drawn from disciplines other than mathematics or composition and from programs other than those in health careers or with external certification or licensure examinations. Responses to my search were, in and of themselves, instructive.

My search elicited a number of requests from people I contacted that I share information with other community college practitioners who are seeking ideas about how to conduct program-level assessments. Clearly there is interest. My search produced examples of program review processes, plans for assessments, and course-level assessments. I also found examples of program-level assessments for nursing graduates and for students taking industry or professional certification examinations in automotive services, Novell, Microsoft, and other vendor-specific subjects. My search did not, however, elicit many examples of program-level assessments in other kinds of programs, assessments that are actually being done rather than just being planned, or assessments that have generated results used by the institution for improving or sustaining program quality. However, I was able to identify a number of interesting assessments, which are described below.

At Rappahannock Community College (Virginia), business faculty developed a portfolio approach to assessing student outcomes (Smith and Crowther, 1996). Members of the program's advisory committee, composed of professionals in the field, reviewed and returned comments on students' portfolios and the professionalism of their projects. Portfolios included a program-specific culminating project, resume, and cover letter written to a specific job advertisement. Comments were returned to students before they left the college. The project provided immediate, concrete feedback to each student, fostered closer ties between advisory committee members and the institution, and gave the faculty insights to keep courses and curricula current. The portfolio project is no longer being used, though faculty have added a new business course that includes interviewing, job readiness skills, cover letters, and resumes.

At Owens Community College (Ohio), the Transportation Technologies Department has developed assessments with corporate partners such as Ford and Caterpillar. Programs are designed to meet corporate expectations, with each program designed for a specific corporate partner, and students are systematically and regularly assessed by faculty and by supervisors in their field experiences. Students completing programs have, by virtue of their course-embedded assessments, demonstrated learning at the program level (Devier, 2002).

At LaGuardia Community College (New York) and at Seattle Central Community College, external researchers examined the academic and social behavior and persistence of new students in learning communities (Tinto, 2000). Tinto and his colleagues used institutional, survey, interview, and observational data to compare students in learning communities with students in similar courses. Findings indicated that students in learning communities were more likely to form self-supporting groups that went beyond the classroom, were more actively engaged in learning even outside the classroom, perceived that the learning community enhanced the quality of their learning, were more likely to persist, and found value in collaboration. For the purposes of this chapter, the multiple methods of assessment employed by Tinto and his team demonstrate the importance of triangulating quantitative and qualitative data and listening to students' stories about their experiences in a program such as a learning community. Learning outcomes clearly extended beyond course subject matter alone.

At Austin Community College (Texas), graduating students in Visual Communication Design (VCD) submit a portfolio containing eight to fifteen examples showing their proficiency in design, illustration, and production art. The college expects that 85 percent of a portfolio must be judged at a level of "competency" for entry-level employment in the field. The student must achieve a score of at least 70 percent to be considered competent. All graduating students are required to attend a pre-portfolio screening with a committee of faculty from the VCD department. Faculty give suggestions about how to improve on presentation and projects in each individual portfolio. Each student is then required to meet with an assigned faculty member to ensure all changes have been completed prior to the professional portfolio review. Professionals from the local visual communication industry review and evaluate students' portfolios based on eight areas identified as most essential for employment success: design, illustration, computer production, Web page design, two-dimensional images, three-dimensional modeling, two-dimensional animation, and three-dimensional animation. Points are awarded based on established numerical criteria; each portfolio's final score can range from 0 to 100 percent. Assessments are conducted annually.

In 2000–01, the overall averages of the portfolios, combining and averaging all of the assessors' scores, was 90.8 percent in the area of graphic design and 73.6 percent in the area of multimedia, for an average of 82.2 percent overall. All but one student achieved a score of competent (70 percent) or better. Based on results, the department established stricter grading criteria for all classes in Visual Communication Design to assure that students are better prepared and meet selected qualifications before enrolling in the portfolio development course.

Oakton Community College (Illinois) provides a final example of good practice in program-level assessment. The college used National Student Clearinghouse data to explore the transfer of students who had earned at least twelve credits in a transfer curriculum and did not report already having a bachelor's degree. The college found that 47.9 percent of students transferred (Bers, 2001). The college also learned that students transferred to a large number of different institutions, indicating a continuing need to be sure information about courses, programs, and articulation is made widely available.

Conclusion

Program-level assessment at community colleges is still in its infancy. Few doubt its importance, and there are examples of good practices. However, challenges remain, and few institutions appear to have constructed ongoing assessment approaches that address learning outcomes at the multicourse or programmatic level. A number of issues continue to perplex assessment champions: agreeing upon the definition of a program in a meaningful way for assessment, identifying students who have completed enough of a program to be reasonably defined as "completers," convincing students to take seriously assessment tests or performances that do not count for grades or graduation, sustaining the energy and resource commitments essential for implementing assessment, and creating assessment approaches that are credible and whose results will be used for program improvement.

This chapter may seem unduly pessimistic. My intent is otherwise. It is to present some realities about program-level assessment, to pique interest in and adoption of a variety of good practices, and to remind readers that program-level assessment can take place in many ways and need not be perfect.

References

Benner, P. "Claiming the Wisdom and Worth of Clinical Practice." *Nursing and Health Care Perspectives,* 1999, *20*(6), 312–319.

Bers, T. H. "Tracking Oakton Transfers: Using The National Student Clearinghouse Enrollment Search." Unpublished paper. Des Plaines, Ill.: Office of Research, Oakton Community College, May 2001.

Boland, D. L., and Laidig, J. "Assessment of Student Learning in the Discipline of Nursing." In C. A. Palomba and T. W. Banta (eds.), *Assessing Student Competence in Accredited Disciplines.* Sterling, Va.: Stylus Publishing, 2001.

Devier, D. H. "Corporate Partnership Student Assessment: The Owens Community College Experience." *Assessment Update,* 2002, *14*(5), 8–10.

National Student Clearinghouse. "Media Relations." http://www.studentclearing-house.org/about/news/default.htm. Accessed Jan. 26, 2004.

Palomba, C. A., and Banta, T. W. *Assessment Essentials: Planning, Implementing, and Improving Assessment in Higher Education.* San Francisco: Jossey-Bass, 1999.

Smith, L. S., and Crowther, E. H. "Portfolios: Useful Tools for Assessment in Business Technology." In T. W. Banta, J. P. Lund, K. E. Black, and F. W. Oblander (eds.), *Assessment in Practice: Putting Principles to Work on College Campuses.* San Francisco: Jossey-Bass, 1996.

Tinto, V. "What Have We Learned About the Impact of Learning Communities on Students?" *Assessment Update,* 2000, *12*(2), 1–2, 12.

TRUDY H. BERS is senior director of research, curriculum, and planning at Oakton Community College in Des Plaines, Illinois.

5

The views of state legislators and agencies that govern higher education must be considered along with institutional perspectives on approaches to assessment of student learning outcomes. This chapter provides a review of performance indicators from twenty-nine recent state reports and discusses their implications for the assessment of student learning outcomes at the campus level.

Implications of State Performance Indicators for Community College Assessment

Joseph C. Burke, Henrik P. Minassians

The 1990s moved accountability for community colleges—and all of higher education—from outcomes assessment to performance reporting. Community college leaders have a vital stake in ensuring that the public reporting of their institutional results reflects their special contribution to higher education. Unfortunately, our study of performance reporting in twenty-nine states suggests that state performance indicators largely ignore the diverse clientele and the specific purposes of community colleges (Burke and Minassians, 2002a). Although performance reporting has become the preferred approach to accountability for higher education in the United States, community college leaders must insist that state reporting measures be modified to reflect the specific purposes of community colleges.

State mandates for assessing student outcomes on campuses flourished in the late 1980s (Boyer, 1987). By the early 1990s, their popularity faded as governors and legislators began replacing this "soft approach" to accountability with performance reporting. States had mandated assessment but allowed campuses to determine their own goals, indicators, and reporting methods. Assessment mandates failed to satisfy accountability on three counts. First, most campuses reacted with external observance or passive resistance. Second, the dual goals of demonstrating external accountability and improving institutional performance seemed incompatible to most academics. Third, assessment tailored to each institution failed to satisfy the

The Ford Foundation supported this study of performance reporting.

desire of governors and legislators to compare campus results (Burke and Minassians, 2002a; Ewell, 1994). "To date," wrote Banta and Borden in 1994, "outcomes assessment . . . for the purpose of demonstrating institutional accountability has produced little information that external decision makers find helpful or satisfying" (p. 96).

State Performance Reporting

Governors, legislators, and higher education coordinating boards advanced performance reporting as an alternative to assessment in assuring accountability. In theory, performance reporting asserted state priorities, adopted indicators assessing their achievement, and allowed comparisons among peer institutions. It rejected the adage that what gets measured is what gets valued and insisted that the real value would come from publicizing the results (Burke and Minassians, 2002b). Performance reporting pledged a shift from processes and inputs to outputs and outcomes. As often happens in public policies, the rhetoric exceeded the reality.

Performance reporting has become the preferred approach to accountability. No fewer than forty-six states now mandate some form of reports (Burke and Minassians, 2002a). They include results for higher education statewide and often for the two- and four-year sectors as well as for individual public institutions. Reporting policies have the avowed purposes of demonstrating external accountability, improving institutional performance, and meeting state needs (Burke and Minassians, 2002b).

Methods

This study uses the indicators from twenty-nine state performance reports issued in 2000 and 2001. It also relies on responses to 349 surveys distributed in 2000 to directors of institutional research at community colleges and four-year institutions in California ($n = 134$), Florida ($n = 35$), South Carolina ($n = 33$), Tennessee ($n = 20$), Texas ($n = 100$), and Wisconsin ($n = 27$). Overall, forty-four percent of those surveyed replied, representing 101 community colleges (42 percent response rate) and 51 baccalaureate institutions (46 percent response rate). The state response rates ranged from a high of 76 percent in South Carolina to a low of 33 percent in California. We chose to survey directors of institutional research because we felt they were the campus officials most knowledgeable about performance indicators and the attitudes of campus groups toward performance reporting.

Chapter Goals

This chapter examines the indicator types, policy values, and the models of excellence implied by state reporting measures for community colleges. It also analyzes the attitudes of directors of institutional research from community colleges and four-year campuses on the appropriateness of twenty-five traditional performance measures. The chapter probes for answers to several questions:

Do the selected indicators and directors' attitudes reflect the community college missions of providing affordable access to job training, baccalaureate transfer, academic remediation, and adult education?

How familiar are community college leaders with state performance report indicators and results?

Do community college leaders use indicators and results from state reports to inform assessment of campus-level student learning outcomes, plan budgets, or perform other vital functions?

What is the effect of using such indicators and results on improving campus policymaking?

The Reporting Indicators

The twenty-nine state reports issued in 2000 and 2001 used a total of 158 generic indicators. Seventeen indicators showed only statewide results for higher education, with no attribution to either community colleges or baccalaureate campuses. Only seven measures applied to community colleges alone. Community colleges shared ninety-seven indicators with baccalaureate institutions, while four-year colleges and universities had twenty-nine distinct indicators (Burke and Minassians, 2002a). Although some of the separate indicators for community colleges, such as adult basic education, job training contracts, and GED pass rates highlighted their special role, the scarcity of community college-specific indicators slights the different missions and clientele of community colleges.

Most Common Indicators

A review of the twenty most common indicators based on the frequency of their use in the twenty-nine state reports, as shown in Table 5.1, suggests the measures were applied fairly evenly to community colleges and four-year institutions. The big differences in job placement and graduation and retention rates reflect the different missions and clientele of each type of institution. Those on student transfer suggest the reluctance of baccalaureate institutions to enforce a joint obligation. Given the mission of community colleges to serve older students, one would have expected a greater difference on enrollment age. The slight disparity on remedial activity or effectiveness is surprising, since states increasingly have moved remediation to community colleges. Although six of the top twenty indicators reflect the special mission and clientele of the community colleges, only student transfer and job placement show sizeable difference in state use.

Table 5.1. Twenty Most Common Indicators in Twenty-Nine State Reports Issued in 2000 and 2001

Indicator	Community Colleges *Number of state reports with indicators*	Baccalaureate Campuses *Number of state reports with indicators*
Student transfer	18	13
Enrollment rate	16	15
Graduation or retention rates	16	21
Tuition and fees	14	15
Job placement	13	5
Remedial activity or effectiveness	11	9
Enrollment, by program type	10	12
Degrees awarded by type and number	9	12
License exams pass rates	9	12
Enrollment residence	8	9
Enrollment trends	8	11
Faculty compensation	8	10
Technology distance learning	8	7
Admin/academic costs/staff	7	8
Enrollment gender	7	8
Financial aid	7	7
Time to degree	7	9
College participation rate	6	5
Enrollment age	6	7
State operating funding	6	7

Indicator Characteristics

The indicators chosen for performance reporting provide clues about policymakers' priorities for community colleges. Their selection raises two key questions: What types of indicators did they favor? What did their choices suggest about their concerns, values, and models of excellence for community colleges? Figures 5.1, 5.2, and 5.3 analyze the 104 indicators used for community colleges compared with the twenty most common measures.

Indicator Types. The indicators fall into four types: inputs, processes, outputs, and outcomes. Multiple designations are used for those that fit more than one classification. *Inputs* are the human, financial, and physical *resources received*. Examples are staffing and funding, student enrollment, and faculty compensation. *Processes* are the *means* of delivering programs, activities, and services. This type includes course requirements, student advisement, and space utilization. *Outputs* involve the *quantity* of products produced. Degrees granted, graduation rates, and time to degree are examples. *Outcomes* represent the *quality* of the benefit or impact of programs, activities, and services on students, states, and society. They include licensure exam scores, job placements, and the results of student, alumni, or employer surveys.

Figure 5.1. Community College Performance Indicator Types

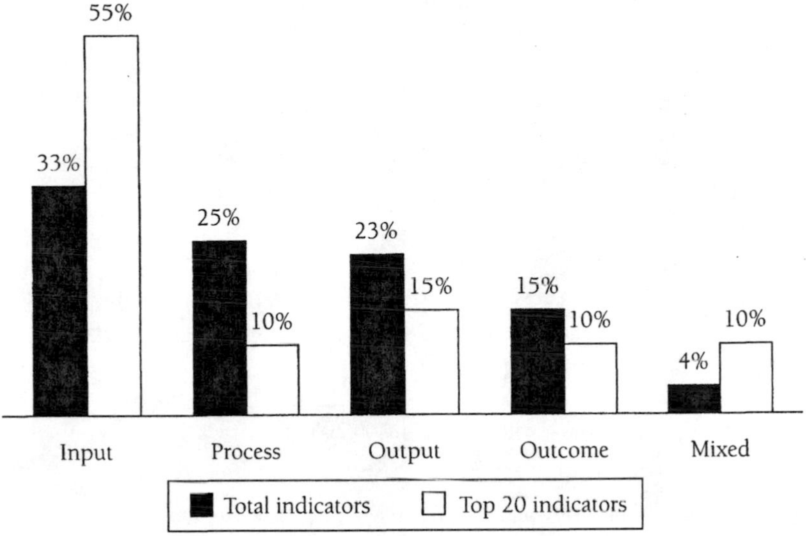

Note: Based on the analysis of twenty-nine state reports issued in 2000 and 2001.

Figure 5.1 belies the rhetoric that performance reporting shifted from the inputs and processes to the outputs and outcomes. The indicator types used in the total number of measures for community colleges exhibit a gradual decline in percentages from inputs to processes, outputs, and outcomes. The top twenty indicators tell a different tale. Inputs garner no less than 55 percent, while outputs fall to 15 percent, and processes and outcomes to 10 percent each. The accent on access and affordability explains the predominance of inputs. Nearly half of the twenty most-used indicators relate to student enrollment, participation, and financial aid. In contrast, just two measures—graduation or retention and degrees awarded—reflect the outputs of degree attainment, while only job placements and licensure test scores constitute outcomes.

Policy Values. The performance indicators reflect the social values of *choice, equity, efficiency,* and *quality* (Richardson, 1994). *Choice* is the capacity to select from a range of options. An example of choice in performance reporting is an indicator allowing colleges to choose one or two measures reflecting their special goals. *Equity* represents the response to the disparities in human needs among different groups. In higher education, equity often relates to the groups a campus admits, graduates, or employs, as expressed in indicators on student, faculty, or staff diversity. *Efficiency* calculates the resources used in relation to the benefits achieved. It includes indicators such as graduation and retention rates and time to degree. *Quality* is achieving or exceeding superior or at least desired standards of performance. Of course,

Figure 5.2. Community College Performance Indicator Value

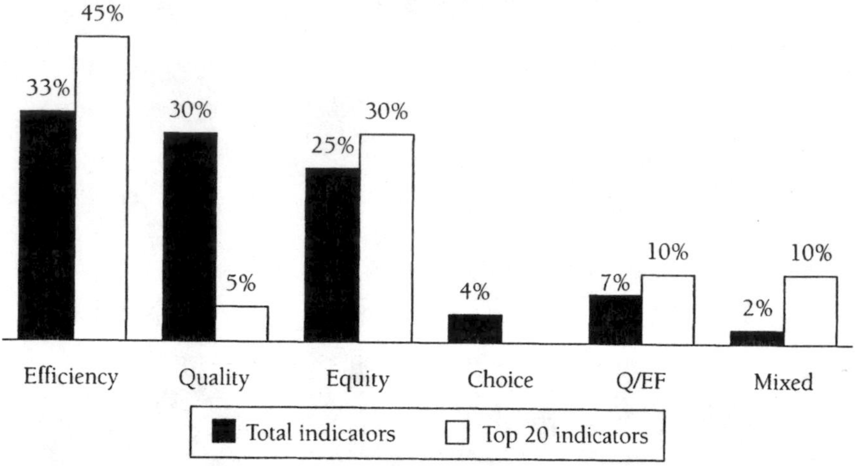

Note: Based on the analysis of twenty-nine state reports issued in 2000 and 2001.

quality is the most elusive of all the values, especially in higher education. Licensure test scores and satisfaction surveys constitute common indicators.

Choice is scarce in the total indicators and non-existent in the top twenty, as shown in Figure 5.2. The total indicators spread fairly evenly across the other policy values. Statistics from the total number of indicators seem to counter the common belief that state policymakers care only for efficiency and not for quality. Again, the top twenty measures show a dramatic shift. Efficiency items—as in graduation rates—soar to 45 percent, while those signifying quality—such as program accreditation—plunge to five percent. The percentages for equity (student, faculty, staff diversity) in both the total and the top indicators represent a welcome surprise, given the recent retreat and continuing attack on affirmative action. The most telling statistic is the scarcity of quality indicators in the twenty most-used measures. Clearly, leaders of both community colleges and four-year campuses have failed to develop robust indicators of student learning outcomes capable of competing with input and process measures of quality and of winning acceptance in the academic community and in state capitols.

Models of Excellence. The indicators selected for reporting also suggest, consciously or unconsciously, models of excellence for public colleges, since they signify the goals and objectives that policymakers perceive as present in successful institutions. As always, models of excellence depend on the eye of the perceiver. The diverse stakeholders of higher education—state officials and the general public, students and their parents, and administrators and professors—mean multiple models.

Figure 5.3. Community College Performance Indicators by Models of Excellence

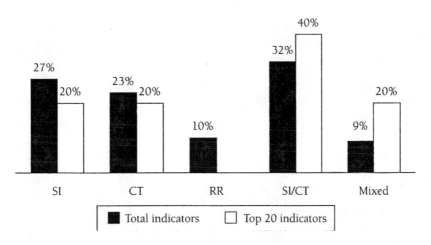

Note: Based on the analysis of twenty-nine state reports issued in 2000 and 2001.

This study uses three models of excellence for colleges and universities in analyzing the performance measures (Burke and Associates, 2002; Burke and Minassians, 2002b). The "Resource and Reputation" model represents a traditional faculty-oriented model based on the inputs of the best students, big budgets, and the best faculty. SAT or ACT scores, faculty compensation, and publications represent indicators suggesting this model. The Strategic Investment is a state-oriented model that calculates costs versus benefits, such as graduation rates or time to degree. The Client or Customer-Centered model suggests responsiveness to the needs of students, states, and society, such as faculty availability to students or satisfaction survey results.

Figure 5.3 suggests that the indicators used for community colleges reflect fairly evenly the Strategic Investment (SI) and the Client Center (CT) models for both the total number and the top twenty measures. As expected, community colleges do not rely heavily on the Resource and Reputation (RR) model, which is often favored by professors and administrators in highly selective colleges and research universities. The surprise is that the highest percent goes to a mixed model combining the benefits of the Strategic Investment and the Customer-Centered models. That mixed model includes measures such as graduation rates, job placements, and community college to baccalaureate transfers, which respond to both state and customer interests. Our research shows the same finding for community colleges in performance funding (Burke and Minassians, 2002b; Burke and Associates, 2002).

Table 5.2. Ranking of Traditional Performance Indicators by Community College Directors of Institutional Research

	Rank	Mean
Pass rates professional licensure exams	1	4.13
Job placements	2	3.98
Graduation or retention rates	3	3.96
Remediation activities or effectiveness	4	3.83
Employer satisfaction survey results	5	3.79
Campus-specific mission indicators	6	3.77
Student satisfaction survey results	7	3.76
Transfer rates from two- to four-year	8	3.75
Enrollment trends	9	3.71
Accredited academic program	10	3.54
Undergraduate student access	11	3.51
Alumni satisfaction survey results	12	3.47
Degrees awarded by type and number	13	3.41
Number of degrees awarded in critical fields	14	3.39
Diversity of students, faculty, and staff	15	3.36
Use of technology/distance learning	16	3.34
K-16 collaboration	17	3.30
Faculty workload	18	3.17
Time to degree	19	3.11
Administrative size or cost	20	3.05
Teacher training	21	3.04
Graduates pursuing advanced degrees	22	2.78
Level of tuition and mandatory fees	23	2.57
Externally sponsored research	24	2.24
SAT/ACT scores of new students	25	2.18

Scale: 1 = Great, 2 = Considerable, 3 = Moderate, 4 = Minimal, 5 = No Extent.

Attitudes Toward Performance Indicators

To assess attitudes on the appropriateness of typical reporting indicators, in 2000 we surveyed directors of institutional research from community colleges and four-year institutions. The twenty-five traditional performance indicators listed in Table 5.2 differ somewhat from the top twenty reporting indicators.

In order of priority, respondents considered pass rates on licensure test scores as the most appropriate indicator, followed by job placement. The surprise was that responses from community colleges rank graduation and retention third in appropriateness, a result that clashed with the idea that this measure is inappropriate for community colleges because many students do not seek degrees. Remediation activities and effectiveness were rated fourth, which was expected.

Familiarity and Use

Reporting information is powerful, but only if it is known and used. Unfortunately, the survey responses reveal that familiarity with report results does not run deep in community colleges and their use on campuses appears less than desired. Directors of institutional research maintain that community college senior officers, deans, and chairs are somewhat more familiar with their states' performance reports than are their counterparts at baccalaureate campuses. Despite this difference, awareness of performance reporting becomes increasing invisible below the level of vice presidents.

Three-quarters of the survey respondents said presidents and vice presidents in community colleges are very familiar or familiar with performance reporting. Only 3 percent of respondents say the senior officers are not familiar with performance reporting. Familiarity plunges below the vice president level. Forty percent of the directors of institutional research from community colleges say their academic deans have little or no familiarity with the reports. More than two-thirds of the directors from community colleges claim their department chairs have little or no familiarity with their state's performance report.

More than 40 percent of the community college institutional researchers assess state performance reports as useful to a great or considerable extent. Slightly fewer than one-quarter said they were useful to a minimal or no extent. Respondents use the report results for campus studies and planning more than for budgeting. Despite the statistics on use, 46 percent of the community college respondents claim that the reports have minimal or no impact on improving campus policymaking.

Findings

This study of state performance reporting for community colleges reveals the following findings:

The reports lack separate indicators that fully reflect the special mission and clientele of community colleges.

Despite the rhetoric about results, because of the focus on access and affordability, the reporting measures stress inputs much more than outputs and outcomes.

Equity measures are prominent in spite of current general reactions against affirmative actions.

The reporting indicators reject the Resource or Reputation model in favor of Strategic Investment, Customer-Oriented, and their mixed model.

Large majorities of the leaders of the divisions and departments most responsible for performance have little or no familiarity with the performance reports.

Performance reports receive moderate to considerable use but have only minimal effect in improving policymaking on campus.

The performance reports become increasingly invisible on campus at the dean and department levels.

Recommendations

Community colleges should have reporting indicators that reflect their distinct goals. State policymakers should include more reporting indicators that reflect the combination of efficiency and quality as complementary, not competing, values. They should also increase the indicators that reflect the mixed model of the Strategic Investment and Client-Centered models, which combines the critical components of costs, benefits, and responsiveness to the needs of students, states, and society. Community colleges should develop a few robust measures of student learning outcomes that are not dependent on selective inputs. Higher education must develop internal performance reports that reach to academic departments that are largely responsible for the most important institutional results.

The last recommendation reflects a fatal problem of performance reporting. Closing the accountability gap requires pushing reporting on some common indicators down to academic departments. State governments fund campus activities, and system and institutional leaders coordinate them, but faculty members in departments educate students. Since performance reporting programs become increasingly invisible on campus below the level of vice president, a system of internal reporting from academic departments on a limited list of core indicators is needed to develop an unbroken chain of performance reporting.

Institutions as well as states and systems need a reporting mechanism to track the source of their successes and shortcomings. The Higher Education Program of the Rockefeller Institute of Government, supported by the Ford Foundation, is currently working to develop a core set of departmental indicators.

Conclusion

Performance reporting has replaced assessment mandates at the state level as the preferred approach to accountability for higher education. Yet the pledge to shift from resource inputs to societal results remains more rhetoric than reality. In many ways, the ideals of performance reporting seem especially suited to the mission of community colleges. Traditionally, they focus on results rather than inputs, and on responsiveness to citizen and community needs rather than resources and reputation.

Reporting higher education results for community colleges and all of higher education has swept the country. *Measuring Up 2000* and *Measuring Up 2002* (National Center for Public Policy and Higher Education, 2000, 2002) grade the fifty states on their comparative achievements. Forty-six states now issue their own reports, as do many two- and four-year systems. Nearly all public colleges or universities also report their performance. Despite all this reporting, doubts remain about performance of higher education in our nation and its states. Patrick Callan, the president of the National Center for Public Policy and Higher Education that issued *Measuring Up,* describes the "national picture of higher education . . . as it serves *all* Americans"—as "one of unevenness and even mediocrity" (National Center for Public Policy and Higher Education, 2002, p. 16).

The mediocre grades for many states in *Measuring Up* raise an intriguing question: How can so much reporting at the levels of the state, system, and institution have so little positive effect on performance? One answer is surprisingly simple: All these reports fail to measure down to academic departments as well as up to states, systems, and institutions. Community colleges that focus on results and on responsiveness to community needs could take the lead in developing departmental indicators that would help higher education measure down as well as up the performance chain.

References

Banta, T. W., and Borden, V.M.H. "Performance Indicators for Accountability and Improvement." In T. W. Banta and V.M.H. Borden (eds.), *Using Performance Indicators to Guide Strategic Decision Making.* New Directions for Institutional Research, no. 82. San Francisco: Jossey-Bass, 1994.

Boyer, C. "Assessment and Outcomes Measurement—View from the States: Highlights of a New ECS Survey and Individual State Profiles." Boulder, Colo.: Education Commission of the States, 1987.

Burke, J. C. *Performance-Funding Indicators: Concerns, Values, and Models for Two- and Four-Year Colleges and Universities.* Albany, N.Y.: The Rockefeller Institute of Government, 1997.

Burke, J. C., and Associates. *Funding Public Colleges and Universities for Performance: Popularity, Problems and Prospects.* Albany, N.Y.: The Rockefeller Institute of Government, 2002.

Burke, J. C., and Minassians, H. P. *Reporting Higher Education Results: Missing Links in the Performance Chain.* New Directions for Institutional Research, no. 116, San Francisco: Jossey-Bass, December 2002a.

Burke, J. C., and Minassians, H. P. *The Preferred "No Cost" Accountability Program: The Sixth Annual Report.* Albany, N.Y.: The Rockefeller Institute of Government, 2002b.

Burke, J. C., and Minassians, H. P. *Performance Reporting: "Real" Accountability or Accountability "Lite": Seventh Annual Survey.* Albany, N.Y.: The Rockefeller Institute of Government, 2003.

Burke, J. C., and Serban, A. M., *Performance Funding for Public Higher Education: Fad or Trend?* New Directions for Institutional Research, no. 97. San Francisco: Jossey-Bass, 1998.

Ewell, P. T. *Assessment and the "New Accountability": A Challenge for Higher Education Leadership.* Denver: Education Commission of the States Working Papers, 1990.

Ewell, P. T. "A Matter of Integrity: Accountability and the Future of Self-Regulation." Nov-Dec. 1994, *Change, 26,* 24–29.

National Center for Public Policy and Higher Education. *Measuring Up 2000: The State-By-State Report Card For Higher Education.* San Jose: National Center For Public Policy and Higher Education, 2000.

National Center For Public Policy and Higher Education. *Measuring Up 2002: The State-By-State Report Card For Higher Education.* San Jose: National Center For Public Policy and Higher Education, 2002.

Richardson, R. C. "Effectiveness in Undergraduate Education: An Analysis of State Quality Indicators." In S. S. Ruppert (ed.), *Charting Higher Education Accountability: A Sourcebook on State-Level Performance Indicators.* Denver: Education Commission of the States, 1994.

JOSEPH C. BURKE is director of the Higher Education Program at the Rockefeller Institute of Government in Albany, New York.

HENRIK P. MINASSIANS is a former research associate with the Higher Education Program at the Rockefeller Institute of Government in Albany, New York.

6

This chapter is designed to acquaint the reader with the context for accreditors' increased emphasis on student learning outcomes as a key indicator of institutional quality and on the use of learning assessment as a key strategy for guiding institutional improvement. It articulates accreditors' expectations for the presentation of evidence that the institution is using student learning outcomes assessment as part of its quality improvement efforts.

The Role of Student Learning Outcomes in Accreditation Quality Review

Barbara A. Beno

In recent years, accreditation standards developed and used by most of the regional accreditors have changed to incorporate the assessment of student learning as a central process in evaluating institutional effectiveness. The incorporation of student learning outcomes into accreditation evaluation processes reflects a decade-long movement in higher education to assess student learning.

This movement itself is both a product of the concern of higher education practitioners with the quality of their own institutional and professional practices and an effort to identify and better address diverse student learning needs. Many community colleges perceive the work to articulate desired student learning outcomes and to assess student learning as likely to lead to greater institutional focus on students. Many faculty, on the other hand, perceive work on student learning as a rewarding means of exploring student learning needs and new pedagogical strategies. Institutions and faculty alike believe that a more directed concern with student learning outcomes will lead to better learning.

Institutional and faculty assessment of student learning has been conducted in the context of an increasing public concern with accountability in higher education. Among the streams of thought feeding the concern with the quality of student learning are the growing demands on limited financial aid funds, growing numbers of students seeking to attend a relatively stable number of higher education institutions, and increased public concern with the role and purpose of higher education in society. This public interest may be termed *accountability*, although the term is often incorrectly used to reflect a singular interest in quantitative measures of student progress through an institution rather than the public's fundamental interest in what students are supposed to learn and how well they are, in fact, learning.

Accreditation is the primary means of quality assessment and assurance used by higher education in the United States. Accrediting agencies have experienced the increasing public concern for accountability of higher education as pressure to focus their own processes for reviewing institutional quality on student outcomes—student progress through the institution as well as student learning. More important, accreditors came to understand that quality review processes that include a focus on student learning draw the accreditation process itself nearer to its true purpose of assessing the quality of education offered by an institution of higher education.

Although each accrediting agency maintains its own standards and process, accreditors nationwide share ideas about the role of student learning outcomes. Almost all of the eight regional accrediting agencies have recently altered their standards and evaluation processes to increase the emphasis on student learning. They have done this while engaged in dialogue with one another about strategies for implementation. In 2001, the eight regional accrediting agencies obtained funding from the Pew Charitable Trusts to conduct a collaborative research study on the use of student learning outcomes in accreditation. This work furthered each regional accreditor's commitment to using student learning as a central part of the accreditation quality review process. Accreditors' work was also assisted by the publication of a Council for Higher Education Accreditation (CHEA) document (Ewell, 2001), which provided accreditors with a terminology and policy framework for incorporating student learning outcomes into accreditation processes.

Accreditation and Student Learning

Accreditation, by design, evaluates institutional quality. Institutional quality is determined by how well an institution fulfills its purposes. From the perspective of accrediting agencies, producing learning is one of the core purposes of an institution of higher education. In assessing institutional quality, accreditors are evaluating the student learning produced by the institution in the context of the institution's own mission, its stated learning objectives, and its identified means of assessing student learning. The challenge to community colleges is to identify the expected student learning outcomes for their own institution in the context of mission and the institution's own curriculum and to develop means of assessing that learning.

Accreditors view their central purpose as improving institutional quality. In this effort, they acknowledge that institutions take time to reach excellence. All accreditors have standards that expect institutions themselves to assess institutional effectiveness regularly, to use the analysis of that assessment to identify and plan needed improvements, to implement those improvements, and to check their impact during another cycle of institutional assessment.

Accreditors have done more than add student learning to the list of indicators of institutional effectiveness. They have recast the meaning of institutional effectiveness to require that institutional assessment and improvement strategies ultimately support learning or result in improved student learning. Community colleges must demonstrate that students achieve the learning results intended and that the institution improves student learning, where needed, over time. The challenge, then, for community colleges is to develop sound methods of assessing student learning. The process of assessing student learning will inevitably cause faculty to explore a variety of forms of pedagogical as well as assessment strategies. Deciding on the most effective strategies for teaching and for assessing learning will require experimentation, careful research, analyses, and time.

Accreditors will require community colleges to collectively attribute meaning to the results of learning assessment and to plan institutional improvements that will result in better learning. A challenge for community colleges is to develop the capacity to discuss what the results of learning assessment mean, to identify ways of improving student learning, and to make institutional commitments to that improvement by planning, allocating needed resources, and implementing strategies for improvement.

The self-study process conducted as part of an accreditation evaluation visit is meant to report on ongoing institutionalized self-evaluation. Maki (2002) notes that institutions too often view the commitment to assessing institutional quality with a compliance mentality rather than with eagerness to explore, with curiosity, questions that are intrinsically important to faculty, administrators, support staff, trustees, members of the public, and accreditors. The questions common to all of those groups include: How well are students learning, after all the college does for and with them? How could we improve learning in order to improve students' lives? Institutional and accreditation engagement with student learning provides all of those groups an opportunity to explore the answers to those questions collectively. Accreditors have incorporated a focus on student learning into accreditation quality review processes in the belief that it will ultimately help improve students' lives.

Ultimately, accreditors and institutions will use information about student learning as well as institutional efforts to improve learning to describe institutional quality in terms that are meaningful to the public—to students, to parents, to employers, and to legislators. That institutional quality will come to be defined in terms that describe the quality of student learning will be a significant departure from the past, when quality was often described in terms of institutional resources or student attainment of benchmarks such as graduation, transfer, or job placement. Given the increasing public interest in the question of what students are learning, institutions and accreditors alike are wise to develop thoughtful, careful, and valid means of assessing learning, talking about the results of assessment, and using the meaning generated through discussion to improve the quality of learning.

Some Practical Guidance for Institutions

When accreditors evaluate community colleges, they will focus on the strength of the institution's own claims that it is fulfilling its educational purpose or mission. Accreditors will need to understand how the college has defined student learning outcomes appropriate to institutional mission and goals, how the college has structured its own processes for evaluating student learning, and how the college planned and implemented changes designed to improve learning. Accreditors will want to examine evidence that the institution is meaningfully engaged in assessing student learning, and they will want to see some evidence of student learning.

Community colleges should be prepared to document institutional efforts with respect to student learning. Following are some suggestions for community colleges preparing to incorporate student learning into their central quality improvement processes as well as preparing for an eventual accreditation team visit.

Document Expected Student Learning Outcomes. Community colleges will need to demonstrate that they have set student learning goals that are appropriate for the course, program, certificate, or degree offered and that conform with the institution's own standards for quality. These goals must also be consistent with higher education standards of quality. Community colleges will want to set clear learning goals that speak to the content and level of learning that students are expected to achieve. These goals should be represented in writing and should be used to inform faculty pedagogy as well as to tell students what is expected of them. Community colleges should be able to present accreditors with written documentation that the expected student learning outcomes have been set and communicated to faculty and students.

Evidence that an institution has set expected learning outcomes might include course syllabi given to students, official course outlines that an institution uses to inform faculty teaching a course, or similar documentation of the expected learning outcomes designed for student services activities or learning support activities. Evidence that an institution has aligned the learning outcomes of a single educational experience (such as a course or a workshop) with the learning goals of a program or culminating degree or certificate includes records of institutional discussions, rubric, charts, or other graphics that show the summative learning goals the institution has defined. Where the process of setting or revising expected learning outcomes has involved important institutional discussion, institutions will also want to document the content of those discussions.

Document Institutional Assessment of Learning. Community colleges need to collect evidence on how well students are learning. Effective assessment will require institutions to design appropriate assessment strategies carefully. Faculty should employ both formative and summative assessment strategies that reflect diverse students' different ways of demonstrating that they have learned. Community colleges should be prepared to demonstrate that the assessment methodologies they have employed to assess learning are valid and reliable. Where institutions are experimenting with different assessments strategies, they should keep some record of experimental results.

Accreditors will evaluate the institution's engagement with assessment of learning. The faculty, staff, and administration of institutions will need to work collectively to evaluate the meaning of assessment results. The accreditors' concern with assessment of student learning is not meant to target individual faculty members, but to stimulate institution-wide engagement with student leaning and institution-wide improvement in learning.

Evidence that an institution might use to demonstrate its assessment efforts includes the assessment instruments themselves, some record of experiments and research on assessment strategies, and any efforts to compile the results of assessment in order to make summative judgments about student learning at the program, certificate, or degree level. Community colleges should also keep a record of the institutional interpretation of the meaning of the assessment results, as well as institutional dialogues that led to that interpretation.

Document Student Learning Outcomes. Community colleges should be able to document that students are meeting the expected learning goals the institution has set. This documentation would take the form of assessment results compiled by individual faculty for the learning experiences they conduct as well as those compiled by program, degree, or certificate. Accreditors will want to see some representative sample of this learning as evidence of institutional quality. Community colleges may want to compile assessment reports by program, certificate, or degree, or to compile examples of student work that show progressive learning, such as in the form of learning portfolios.

Document Use of Assessment Results for Institutional Improvements. The collection and use of student learning outcomes data are meant to be a collective effort used to inform institutional efforts to improve quality of education. They should not be the sole responsibility of individuals or a separate assessment function. Accreditors will evaluate the institution's degree of engagement with the assessment of learning. Community colleges should be able to demonstrate that there is institution-wide understanding of educational quality as measured in a way that includes student learning outcomes, and that there are institutionalized commitments to improving learning. Community colleges should be prepared to demonstrate the ways in which assessment and interpretation are used institution-wide to inform planning and implement changes.

Evidence of the ways in which institutions use the results of assessment to improve learning include documentation of important institutional discussions; documentation that shows how plans to improve learning are incorporated into institutional evaluation and improvement processes, such as program review or educational or strategic planning; and evidence that the plans to improve student learning are implemented over time. Evidence might also include policies that emphasize the use of student learning assessment in institutional evaluation, planning, or funding processes.

Accreditors will definitely seek information about how well institutional members understand the institution's own assessment strategies and the results of assessment. Individuals on campus should be prepared to field questions from visiting team members about student learning assessment and institutional meanings and commitments attached to the results of assessment.

How Some Institutions Are Addressing Student Learning Outcomes

Many higher education institutions have already developed strategies for assessing student learning and are using that assessment to improve institutional quality. Alverno College (Wisconsin), the most well-known institution in the student learning movement, has been assessing student learning for nearly twenty years. Its staff has provided a good deal of leadership to the national student learning assessment movement. The California State University at Monterey Bay, a relatively new institution, was designed to provide institutional processes that ensure adequate feedback from assessment of student learning outcomes to institutional processes for decision making.

For the last several years, the American Association for Higher Education (AAHE) has been offering workshops on assessment that bring experienced practitioners together with institutional teams that are just beginning to develop an institutional approach to defining and assessing student learning. Two of the regional accrediting agencies are cosponsoring AAHE workshops for institutions in their respective regions.

At Mesa Community College (Arizona), staff designed an approach to assessing general education outcomes and using the results of assessment to improve curriculum, instruction, and learning. The college established seven areas of learning for its general education program: communication, problem solving and critical thinking, numeracy, arts and humanities, scientific inquiry, information literacy, and cultural diversity. In each of these seven areas, the college designed general education outcomes that are each measured with a different assessment tool. The college assesses students enrolled in general education classes at the beginning of study and at the point of completion of general education, providing data on the value added through the general-education experience. Assessment is done during an annual spring assessment week in which selected classes are asked to forgo instruction and instead allow the general-education assessment to be administered to students. A faculty committee interprets assessment results and uses them to develop themes for interdisciplinary faculty work and development over the subsequent years to enhance curriculum and pedagogy in order to improve learning (Mee, 2004).

Colleges and universities that develop student learning outcomes for programs soon encounter the challenge of ensuring that the courses that make up a program of study result in the cumulative learning outcomes intended for the program. One solution is to map the learning outcomes to the various courses that a student takes to complete a program. The Rose-Hulman Institute of Technology has developed a form that includes questions to ask course instructors to identify whether a specific learning outcome is covered in their course and the degree to which it is covered:

Is the outcome explicitly stated as an outcome for the course?
Are students asked to demonstrate their competence through course work that is assessed by the instructor?
Do students receive formal feedback on their mastery of this learning outcome from the instructor (Rogers, 2004)?

Answers to these questions are used to ensure that a curriculum offers appropriate opportunities to learn and practice specific skills associated with the program's expected learning outcomes.

One of the purposes of assessing learning outcomes at the programmatic or institutional level is to provide the institution with feedback that it can use to improve educational quality. Accreditors increasingly ask that community colleges demonstrate a focus on student learning as well as a culture in which data and analyses are used to evaluate institutional quality and develop strategies for improvements. Community colleges face the challenge of gathering information that can foster appropriate discussion and improvement of institutional quality among their internal constituencies. Many institutions have developed Web-based approaches to sharing assessment data and developing collective knowledge for institutional discussions of quality. A good example of this practice can be found at Portland State University's Web site.

A Timeline for Developing Institutional Culture and Practice

Accreditors recognize that institutions will take time to develop a culture and practice that support explication of expected student learning outcomes at all appropriate levels, assessment of student learning, institution-wide capacity to discuss the results of assessment, and the ability to attribute meaning to results in order to inform practice. The regional accrediting agencies, in their own discussions as well as communications to their membership, have suggested a time frame for full implementation of between ten and fifteen years. As community colleges prepare to engage with student learning assessment in the comprehensive manner described above, they should acknowledge the size of the task and anticipate having to work on this effort over many years.

Most community colleges will experience a comprehensive accreditation review within the next ten years. They should be aware that accreditors expect to find them in the process of developing new institutional practices around the assessment of learning, but they will not expect most institutions to have developed their capacity fully. Each college should seek advice from its accrediting agency on what is expected at its next accreditation and know that it will be important to have accomplished some substantial work by the time of the review. Institutions should also know that accreditors themselves are newly engaged with the assessment of student learning. Accreditors will appreciate learning from community colleges the strategies institutions used to explore this way of examining and improving institutional quality. Although they will ultimately make judgments about institutional quality, accreditors see themselves as partners with institutions in discovering what we can all do to improve both learning and students' lives.

References

Ewell, P. *Accreditation and Student Learning Outcomes: A Proposed Point of Departure*. A CHEA Occasional Paper, Council for Higher Education Accreditation, 2001.

Maki, P. L. "Developing an Assessment Plan to Learn about Student Learning." Prepublication version of an article for the *Journal of Academic Librarianship*, January 2002.

Mee, G. "Assessment of Student Learning in General Education: A Case Study." Presentation at Building Learner-Centered Institutions: Developing Strategies for Assessing and Improving Student Learning, Western Association of Schools and Colleges and American Association of Higher Education Workshop, January 2004.

Rogers, G. "Introduction and Overview." Presentation at Building Learner-Centered Institutions: Developing Strategies for Assessing and Improving Student Learning, Western Association of Schools and Colleges and American Association of Higher Education Workshop, January 2004.

BARBARA A. BENO *is the executive director of the Accrediting Commission for Community and Junior Colleges, Western Association of Schools and Colleges.*

7

Online education has become deeply embedded in the offerings of most community colleges. This chapter discusses the challenges, models, and approaches to conducting assessment of student online learning and establishing outcomes for online education.

Assessment of Online Education: Policies, Practices, and Recommendations

John Milam, Richard A. Voorhees, Alice Bedard-Voorhees

Community colleges were among the earliest adopters of distance learning technology and their enrollments in this area continue to grow. According to a National Center for Education Statistics study, 92 percent of all community colleges were engaged in distance education in 2000–2001, serving an estimated 1.5 million students and representing 48 percent of total distance education enrollments among Title IV institutions. These enrollments represent more than occasional classes. More than 520 associate degree programs and 430 certificate programs offered by community colleges can be completed totally at a distance using online technologies (Waits and Lewis, 2003).

The wave of online education certainly spells convenience for students as well as an opportunity for community colleges to rejuvenate themselves by exploring a new instructional paradigm. However, the drum beat for accountability and stewardship of dollars has not subsided in the United States, even during the past several years, when states have been unable to provide stable resources to public higher education. The result is that community colleges will need to continue their leadership in online education by developing and nurturing strategies that assess these efforts.

In some ways, determining what student learning occurs in an online environment is straightforward. However, it is very difficult to analyze the quality or the developmental, critical, and reflective dimensions of online student learning. The emergence of online education forced educators to rethink the total role of higher education institutions in producing the entire

NEW DIRECTIONS FOR COMMUNITY COLLEGES, no. 126, Summer 2004 © Wiley Periodicals, Inc.

range of student learning. Eaton (2001a) explains that "distance education challenges some fundamentals of the academic work and the politics of American higher education—thereby challenging some related features of quality assurance and self-regulation" (p. 3). Unfortunately, the clues that point institutions down pathways to documenting student learning have been neither numerous nor clear.

Shavelson and Huang (2003) describe the current state of assessment as a "frenzy to find something to test college students with" (p. 11). Community college educators have much to gain by a reasoned response to the need to assess online education. This chapter attempts to make sense of this frenzy by examining policy, practice, and logistics in assessing online education and services. While it is our opinion that the current practice of online assessment falls mostly short of the "ideal," recent progress in methodology and technology is encouraging and may foretell significant future progress. Discussion of the interrelated issues of student support services and cost are beyond the scope of this chapter.

Assessment Issues in Policy Research

Unfortunately, there is relatively little empirical research to guide deep policy discussions about assessing online education. Typically, those writing policy identify only the broadest of issues; policy then quickly devolves into requirements to compare and contrasting online educational outcomes with those produced in land-based classrooms. Russell's (1999) early conclusion that there is "no significant difference" between the two delivery methods regardless of the technology used remains widely untested through rigorous application of research design. Despite recent advances in statistical control, the general conclusion that there is "not a difference in the selected learning outcomes" (Meyer, 2002a, p. 2) has assumed almost mantra-like qualities among most online educators. Proponents of "no significant difference" may be correct (Meyer, 2002b). However, a general absence of carefully developed definitions, appropriate research methodology, and replicable results suggests that the case is difficult to make unequivocally.

Still, the debate whether online is inferior, the same, or even superior to land-based education may be the wrong debate. Eaton (2001a) explains that standards and guidelines in distance learning "tend to focus on the similarities between site-based education and electronically based education, paying less attention to the differences between the two approaches to teaching and learning" (p. 3). However, the online paradigm holds that learning itself may be different in an online environment and, if that is true, then the methodology for measuring it should also be different or should measure those things that are, in fact, different.

The policy pendulum now appears to be swinging from comparative analyses toward recognizing that online education should be assessed on its own merits. Obscuring these efforts, however, is a dearth of evidence.

Anecdotes, one-shot case studies, and control-treatment group research designs that ignore external variance can lead only to partial conclusions with limited generalizability beyond the students from which they were drawn. Several large-scale organizations make heavy use of control and treatment groups, where participation in online instruction is the treatment and non-participation the ultimate control variable. Such techniques satisfy fundamental issues in basic research design when extraneous variables can be controlled. However, most external variables are not easily controllable except with sophisticated research design. Sadly, the classic treatment and control group research design fails to account for the influence of external variables on complex phenomena, including student learning. The result ignores the multiplicity of factors that might influence learning, thereby masking the "true" differences produced by online courses. Voorhees characterizes the preoccupation with simplistic research designs that exclude complex phenomena as "two variable models hoping to explain a multivariate world" (2003, n.p.).

The simplicity of the classical research designs makes them very attractive to policymakers. Fortunately, there are several initiatives that address previous policy research shortcomings in ways that may be helpful. The Andrew W. Mellon Foundation sponsored the Cost Effective Uses of Technology in Teaching (CEUTT) program, recognizing that previous research disregarded a number of important factors including curriculum taught, types of technology used, student and faculty familiarity with technology, classroom size, and other factors. "Unfortunately, there is a dearth of such studies or analyses in these areas, despite a long history of scholarship in educational technology" (Fisher, 2001, p. 17). The Pew Grant Program in Course Redesign also focused on decreasing costs—especially by demonstrating the efficacy of large course sections—while increasing the quality of online learning (Twigg, 2003). The central contribution of these projects is their recognition that assessing student learning is not simple and that assessment techniques appropriate to online environments need further refinement.

Accrediting agencies also set online assessment policy by asking whether institutional processes are in place to routinely evaluate the quality of distance learning based on evidence of student achievement. These expectations are at the accreditation forefront, although clear guidelines that would prescribe levels of evidence are conspicuously absent. Many institutions have turned to competencies as a framework for quantifying student learning. The Council for Higher Education Accreditation (CHEA), for example, recognizes that "corporations and other employers demand outcomes to confirm that prospective employees possess carefully delineated job skills" (Eaton, 2001b, p. 2). Using the experience of Western Governors University as a model, CHEA asks "whether competencies are a useful means of addressing outcomes in an accreditation review" (Eaton, 2001b, p. 2). In general, competencies were found to be a helpful framework, though their use across higher education is less than universal.

The obstacles to using competencies include a lack of definitional precision. Terkla (2001), for example, found that regional accreditors describe their expectations for measuring learning outcomes differently. She argues that most standards suggested by the regional accrediting agencies generally encompass what should be required of colleges, but there is little guidance about how to measure the competencies or units of learning that they imply or even what those competencies are. It is ironic that regional accreditors suggest that institutions produce favorable assessment results when the knowledge base that might drive such accreditation decisions, especially the measurement of student learning, has not been fully informed by practice.

Assessment Issues in Practice

The indisputable touchstone for practice and quality in online education is the Western Cooperative for Educational Telecommunications' *Best Practices for Electronically Offered Degree and Certificate Programs* (WCET, 2002). The quality principles therein have been adopted widely, republished, and incorporated into successive versions. The document recommends that community colleges "conduct sustained, evidence-based and participatory inquiry as to whether distance learning programs are achieving objectives. The results of such inquiry are used to guide curriculum design and delivery, pedagogy, and educational processes, and may affect future policy and budgets and perhaps have implications for the institution's roles and mission" (WCET, 2002, p. 12).

Where, then, does this journey begin for community college practitioners? Here we identify the obstacles and opportunities that beset the assessment of online education.

Physical Versus Virtual Dynamics

The largest issue confronting online assessment is that of the dynamics that occur when the instructor and learner do not share the same immediate space. "Assessment and measurement become even more critical in the absence of the face-to-face interactions that enable teachers to use informal observation to gauge student response, obtain feedback, and progress toward goals" (Pennsylvania State University, 1998, n.p.). At the same time, as Sullivan (2003) explains, "Online students get to know their teachers and fellow classmates with some of the white noise of social conditioning filtered out—and this kind of learning experience can be quite exhilarating" (p. 2). This situation was put in context by an online student who wrote, "One positive point for students about learning online is that we do not have to face each other in a classroom atmosphere and be intimidated by looks, weight, height, or personalities" (Sullivan, 2003, p. 2).

Lack of face-to-face contact with students invites the use of proximal assessment measures that may not be necessary in a land-based class. For example, the use of online quizzes, multiple-choice questionnaires, or written assignments and problem-based exercises sent by e-mail may be handled in other ways in a traditional class. Many believe that the assessment process should be as rich as the learning process and should be a transparent process for the student. An allied concern is that of the validity of the assessment. For example, how does one properly assess the impact of a speech that perhaps is only observed through a Web camera rather than in front of an audience? Moreover, how does a faculty member ensure that the person submitting the assessment task is indeed the student?

In fully online environments, multiple measures, formative and summative assessments over the course timeline, and electronic interaction with the learner are sound assessment practices. Because the learner and instructor are not in close proximity, multiple measures are necessary to authenticate the instruction and to provide alternatives to face-to-face discussions. Angelo and Cross (1993) and Diamond (1998) have illustrated assessment tools that lend themselves to multiple measures and that can assist instructors to overcome the problems raised by lack of physical proximity. Courseware is a software application that provides instructional delivery by allowing the user to determine the order and pace of delivery and resulting learning options. Salmon (2002) of Open University builds on Biggs (1999) to define alignment between learning and assessment in an online learning environment as a process of using courseware tools to integrate assessment of the environmental operations and include assessment activities that are "reflective and collaborative" (Salmon, 2002, p. 90).

A Role for Competencies

A recent National Postsecondary Education Cooperative report on competency-based initiatives provides several "strong principles" for assessing and strengthening student learning (Jones, Voorhees, and Paulson, 2002). Among these is the principle that "assessment results are clear and reported in a meaningful way so that all relevant stakeholders fully understand the results" (p. 29). The report introduces basic information about the construction and use of competency assessments and includes the results of eight case studies of competency-based programs. Perhaps the largest contribution of this work for assessment practice is a definition of competency as "the combination of skills, abilities, and knowledge needed to perform a specific task" (p. 7). Institutions can use this basic definition to determine what competencies are offered across their whole curriculum, including online classes.

Western Governors University (WGU, Utah) has been a leader in the measurement of learning. Theirs are degree domains rather than course measurements. Domains consist of a mix of higher- and lower-level competencies, depending on what is appropriate to developing expertise for the awarded degree. WGU makes heavy use of multiple measures, including commercial instruments that have been cross-referenced to competencies, and custom-designed assessment banks and tasks (Testa and Bedard-Voorhees, 1999). WGU offers competency-based associate degree programs that build on knowledge, skills, and experience from work and life. Jones, Voorhees, and Paulson (2002) describe individual competencies as the "basic building blocks of WGU degrees" and the "smallest unit of describable skill or knowledge" (p. 136). Students work with an advisor or mentor to document and evaluate what they know. As at many two-year institutions, preparedness for college-level competencies is measured with a placement assessment. An Academic Action Plan is developed specific to the student's needs, with timelines for sitting for assessments and progressing toward a credential. An assessment battery of instruments and types is used, including some built to WGU requirements and some from third parties, to measure each domain of knowledge. There is a "coverage chart" that matches performance descriptions with assessment instruments. Each battery of assessment must include "authentic performance tasks" and allow for "different contextual manifestations of the ability" (p. 141).

While WGU's initial expectation was that enough existing tests would be available on the market to measure the required competencies, they found that "existing assessments cover only a piece of any given domain. The result is that existing assessments must be configured in a patchwork to create the assessment batteries" (Jones, Voorhees, and Paulson, 2002, p. 144). The format and style of different tests, as well as "legal maneuvering among the various testing and assessment groups" (p. 146) also cause "unique problems" for WGU (p. 145). Even so, the long-lasting contribution of WGU to higher education is in providing the fundamental building block for assessment.

The University of Phoenix also focuses on core competencies when designing online courses. This focus, they say, "enables us to benchmark and assess students' progress both in the core competencies of their study and in those broader areas (such as critical thinking) that form the bigger picture of our educational programs. These competencies are assessed through matched pre- and post-tests administered to students as they enter and exit their major course of study" (De Alva and Slobodzian, 2001, p. 17).

McKnight (2002) presents a useful checklist for faculty to use to construct online courses that embrace the use of specific outcome statements. Similarly, Bedard-Voorhees (2001) presents a useful checklist for faculty and administrators to use in implementing and evaluating competency-based instruction that can be utilized for new courses in both distance and land-based modes.

Changing Faculty Roles and Curriculum

Another important assessment issue is the impact of changing faculty roles on the learning experience. Faculty roles are sometimes simplified in two online learning motifs, "sage on the stage" versus the "guide on the side."

While the shift from delivering pedagogy to facilitating student learning is fundamental, other changes in faculty roles are less explored.

Use of competencies allows connecting courses with related outcomes into modules or chunks and reworking traditional faculty roles in design and delivery of course material. For example, online course content frequently is re-used. Since it is cheaper to use part-time faculty to teach an online course after it has been developed, these courses are often taught without the original faculty member's ongoing involvement. Some argue that no online course can be as good as it was when it was delivered by the faculty who created it. Others counter that as long as the course competencies are delivered in ways that respond to learner needs and that those competencies can be measured, it matters little who is the instructor of record. The days of faculty being able to be involved in all aspects of the delivery of a course are numbered at some institutions. However, whether the original faculty are present or not in course delivery, it appears critical that faculty expertise be used to "define the learning outcomes, the applications of that learning, the content, and potential difficulties that students may encounter" (Twigg, 2001, p. 9).

Traditional roles melt away in an online environment. Unfortunately, learning theory, instructional design theory, and practical assessment are not common knowledge among most faculty and administrators. The promise and challenge of building stronger assessment for many institutions will include professional development in these areas. For example, the Community Colleges of Colorado Online now offers faculty the opportunity to take an online workshop on summative and formative assessment techniques called Measuring What Matters Online (Colorado Community Colleges Online, 2001). Faculty learn to identify the elements that allow students to demonstrate their acquisition of identified course competencies. Such elements may be presented in the form of quizzes, papers, projects, or online discussions (Bedard-Voorhees, 2001). These online courses also provide rubrics for the assessment of the non-objective tasks, including discussions.

Assessment Tools

Advantages and disadvantages of case studies, discussions, software simulations, electronic portfolios, and self-assessments are examined in the ERIC Clearinghouse on Adult, Career, and Vocational Education (ERIC-ACVE, 2000) *Practitioner File,* "Assessing Learners Online." The importance of portfolios in online education is well documented. See the special Web site on this topic entitled Electronic Portfolios: Resources for Higher Education (AAHE, 2004).

Online (or electronic) portfolios can feature multiple examples of student work, can be rich in context, can offer opportunities for selection and assessment, and can offer a look at development over time. Online portfolios allow institutions to become both evaluative and consultative, with continuous internal and external communication (Cambridge, 2000). They "create a living showcase" of educational, career, and personal achievement (eFolio Minnesota, 2004).

The growing sophistication of online assessment tools makes continuous assessment much more practical. Institutions such as Rio Salado College in the Maricopa Community College District in Phoenix "are known for building a continuous assessment loop through the collection, analysis, and dissemination of data" (Twigg, 2001, p. 30).

Measuring Engagement

A large task for effective assessment in an online environment is measuring student and faculty engagement. Whether or not students are motivated to participate within a course, most colleges require a certain level of involvement, in part to assure that students and faculty are making a corresponding effort to engage in course content commensurate to the effort expended in land-based courses. The WCET best practices document is very specific in its review of expectations for Internet-based courses: "The importance of appropriate interaction (synchronous or asynchronous) between instructor and students and among students is reflected in the design of the program and its courses, and in the technical facilities and services provided" (WCET, 2002, p. 550). There is some evidence that, beyond participation in classes, students are less likely to discuss academic goals and career plans with online instructors than with instructors of traditional classes (Obler, Gabriner, and Slark, 2000).

Helping students feel that they are a part of a learning community is critical to persistence, learning, and satisfaction. In many cases, human contact is necessary for more than just learning content. Encouragement, praise, and assurance that they are on the right learning path are also critical feedback components that help students get through rough times and keep on working. Knowing that someone is there to help when they get stuck and to get them moving again gives students the confidence that they can succeed.

In assessing interaction, feedback, and discussion, evaluators should measure whether students perform substantive work and have periodic interactions with other students and with the instructor. Evidence should be generated from weekly class participation, postings, and submitted work. There should be feedback from multiple sources, including peer feedback that is meaningful and constructive. There should be clear methods for evaluating performance in online discussions, and participation should be reflected in the course grade or point system (Jansak, 2003). Faculty expectations for student engagement should be fully embedded in course syllabi. At the same time, students should expect timely feedback, and this should be incorporated in faculty review (see, for example, Colorado Community Colleges Online, 2001).

Another evaluative benchmark is whether the course is designed to require group work by students. Research has shown that students in distance education take on the role of teacher more often than do students in traditional classrooms. A sense of community is promoted as an "ongoing, long-term relationship" through such efforts as encouraging study groups, providing student directories, and including online students in publications and events (WCET, 2002). There are many forms of collaboration besides student-to-student and faculty-to-student interaction. Thach and Murphy (2002) explore what is termed the "collaboration continuum," which includes student-to-student, class-to-class, and institution-to-institution collaboration. Commercial course-management software packages such as WebCT and Blackboard are able to track students' time on task online, including participation in discussions and in various parts of the course. This feature can be used to gauge student engagement in a basic, time-on-task mode.

Online courses are not a good match for all students. Many students do not understand the demands of taking an online course and how their learning styles might, or might not, be supported by online instruction. Students should be informed about what is involved in taking an online course, including the technical skills needed, the time frame for course completion, access to libraries and support services, and expectations for online interaction with faculty and other students.

As WCET's *Best Practices* document (2002) states, it is important that institutions assist "the prospective student in understanding independent learning expectations as well as the nature and potential challenges of learning in the program's technology-based environment" (p. 10). The American Federation of Teachers' (AFT) publication "Guidelines for Good Practice" promotes the standard that "students must fully understand course requirements and be prepared to succeed" (AFT, 2001, p. 19).

Student Satisfaction and Retention

Student satisfaction and retention rates in online courses are sometimes misused as proxies for assessment of student learning. Clearly, student satisfaction is a necessary ingredient for effective participation in online education, but it is not synonymous with student learning outcomes. Still, in some circles, it is the sine qua non for determining the success of online efforts. Retention is also used frequently as a measure of learning outcomes, and while there is some legitimate reason to think that those who are not retained cannot be educated, it simply cannot be equated to student learning. A national assessment organization recognized by the Distance Education and Training Council (DETC) specifies that institutions must show "that students are satisfied with the instructional and educational services" and that "students complete their studies at rates that compare favorably to those at similar courses/programs" (DETC, 2004, p. 5). The incompleteness of satisfaction as an outcome argues for including information about student goals, institutional mission, course objectives, and technology as intervening or perhaps antecedent variables.

Student motivation is a strong determinant of the outcomes and success of learning, especially in online education (Elwert and Hitch, 2002; Obler, Gabriner, and Slark, 2000). A recent study of students enrolled in online courses throughout the Virginia Community College System indicates that student learning outcomes, specifically related to student motivation, influence successful completion rates. One of the fundamental concepts of Ford's Motivational Systems Theory (1992) is that emotional activation has little impact if a goal is dormant. Building on Ford's theory, Jamison (2003) finds that capability beliefs, responsive environment, goal activation, goal alignment, human respect, goal salience, emotional activation, multiple goals, and feedback are robust predictors of student completion.

Conclusion

It is not likely that the foregoing issues for practice will ever disappear. Certainly, several have no easy solution. Community colleges can position themselves to demonstrate quality learning outcomes with online assessment. We believe that this goal is met when community colleges make an initial assessment of students' current academic competencies and learning style, learning activities are of a high quality, there is opportunity to integrate each student's competencies within the online course or program in which they are enrolled, assessment is ongoing and systematic, and interaction is readily available to supplement learning outcomes.

A specific distance learning assessment plan should be developed and synchronized with an institution's overall assessment plan. A written plan requires that the institution as a whole focus on its online learning program. An institutional plan should also call for multiple methods to assess online education while ensuring that standards are in place for comparisons; that evaluations of program effectiveness are data-driven and include enrollment and cost information; and that intended student outcomes are reviewed regularly to make sure they are clear, useful, and appropriate (Phipps and Merisotis, 1999, 2002; Twigg, 2001).

Academically qualified personnel should be responsible for the plan and process of assessment as well as for the incorporation of the results into the curriculum. This is an important point stressed specifically by the Southern Association of Colleges and Schools (SACS), CHEA, WCET, and the AFT. Faculty should assume responsibility for and exercise oversight over distance education (SACS, 2001, p. 1). Stated more explicitly in its distance education guidelines for good practice, AFT recommends that "Faculty must retain academic control" (AFT, 2001, p. 1).

It is clear in reviewing accrediting standards, best practices, and current research about measuring success in online student outcomes that there are a number of issues to which institutions need to give close attention. From faculty roles to competency-based initiatives and knowledge chunks, many different pieces of the assessment puzzle must be brought together in the broader context of the institutional mission of access and affordability. This requires considerable expertise in assessment and program evaluation, and a wider appreciation of the potentials of online education. Institutions would do well to determine whether such knowledge and skills exist on their campuses or whether considerable professional development is required to ensure that online assessment occurs in meaningful ways.

Community colleges with relatively limited resources for assessment still find that accreditation hinges on effective delivery of online courses and that regional accreditors are increasingly focused on the implementation of best practices and ongoing assessment with a variety of methods. Comparison studies have been shown to be of little utility except in better understanding the process and measurement of learning. Community colleges are doing many things well with online education, usually with limited information about the relationship between cost and quality. It is critical that they not become complacent with acceptable rates of student satisfaction with online courses, but continue to assess the dynamic, changing, and challenging nature of this relatively new paradigm of higher education.

It is important to incorporate principles about student motivation and engagement, to document collaboration and interaction, and to understand how the online environment facilitates a sense of community and inclusion. Community college leaders will become more and more aware of how traditional course structures and formats are outdated. With the growing focus on knowledge management, there is increasing interest in providing knowledge chunks in different delivery formats, documenting and assessing their impact through the use of core and specific competencies.

References

American Association of Higher Education. "Electronic Portfolios: Emerging Practices for Students, Faculty, and Institutions." http://webcenter1.aahe.org/electronicportfolios/index.html. Accessed Feb. 10, 2004.

American Federation of Teachers. *A Virtual Revolution: Trends in the Expansion of Distance Education.* Washington, D.C.: American Federation of Teachers, 2001.

American Federation of Teachers. "Guidelines for Good Practice." 2001. http://www.aft.org/higher_ed/downloadable/distance.pdf. Accessed May 16, 2004.

Angelo, T., and Cross, K. P. *Classroom Assessment Techniques.* San Francisco: Jossey-Bass, 1993.

Bedard-Voorhees, A. "Creating and Implementing Competency-Based Learning Models." In R. A. Voorhees (ed.), *Measuring What Matters: Competency-Based Learning Models in Higher Education.* San Francisco: Jossey-Bass, 2001.

Biggs, J. "What the Student Does: Teaching for Enhanced Learning." *Higher Education Research and Development,* 1999, 18(1), 57–75.

Cambridge, B. (ed.). *Electronic Portfolios: Emerging Practices in Student, Faculty, and Institutional Learning.* Washington, D.C.: American Association for Higher Education, 2000.

Colorado Community Colleges Online. *Measuring What Matters Online.* Online workshop. 2001. http://www.ccconline.org/faculty/training_schedule.htm. Accessed Feb. 10, 2004.

De Alva, J. K., and Slobodzian, K. A. "University of Phoenix: A Focus on the Customer." In C. Twigg (ed.), *Innovations in Online Learning: Moving Beyond No Significant Difference.* Troy, N.Y.: Center for Academic Transformation, Rensselaer Polytechnic Institute, 2001.

Diamond, R. M. *Designing and Assessing Courses and Curricula: A Practical Guide.* San Francisco: Jossey-Bass, 1998.

Distance Education and Training Council. *Accreditation Standards.* Washington, D.C.: The Distance Education and Training Council, 2004. http://www.detc.org/acreddit Handbk.html. Accessed Feb. 10, 2004.

Eaton, J. *Distance Learning: Academic and Political Challenges for Higher Education Accreditation.* Washington, D.C.: Council of Higher Education Accreditation, 2001a.

Eaton, J. *The Competency Standards Project: Another Approach to Accreditation Review.* Washington, D.C.: Council of Higher Education Accreditation, 2001b.

eFolio Minnesota. *eFolio Minnesota: Your Electronic Showcase.* Minnesota State Colleges and Universities, 2004. http://www.efoliomn.com. Accessed Feb. 10, 2004.

Elwert, B., and Hitch, L. (eds.). *Motivating and Retaining Adult Learners Online.* Essex Junction, Vt.: GetEducated.com, 2002.

ERIC Clearinghouse on Adult, Career, and Vocational Education (ERIC-ACVE). "Assessing Learners Online." *Practitioner File.* http://www.cete.org/acve/docs/pfile03. htm. Accessed June 7, 2004. Columbus: ERIC Clearinghouse on Adult, Career, and Vocational Education, 2000.

Fisher, S. *Teaching and Technology: Promising Directions for the Foundation's Support of Research on Online Learning and Distance Education in the Selective Institutions.* New York: Andrew W. Mellon Foundation, 2001.

Ford, M. E. *Motivating Humans: Goals, Emotional, and Personal Agency Beliefs.* Newbury Park, Calif.: Sage Publications, 1992.

Jamison, T. M. "Ebb from the Web: Using Motivational Systems Theory to Predict Student Completion of Asynchronous Web-based Distance Education Courses." Unpublished doctoral dissertation, George Mason University, 2003.

Jansak, K. E. "Gagne: Longitudinal Dimensions of Learning: The 9 'Events' or 'Stages.'" Notes from an Instructional Design for Web-Intensive Courses Workshop. Portsmouth, Ohio: Shawnee State University, 2003. http://www.edison.cc.oh.us/online/gagne.pdf. Accessed Feb. 10, 2004.

Jones, E. A., Vorhees, R. A., and Paulson, K. "Defining and Assessing Learning: Exploring Competency-Based Initiatives." NCES 2002–159. Washington, D.C.: U.S. Department of Education, National Center for Education Statistics, 2002.

McKnight, R. *Principles of Online Design Checklist.* Florida Gulf Coast University: Faculty Development and Support, 2002. http://www.fgcu.edu/onlinedesign/checklist.html. Accessed Feb. 10, 2004.

Meyer, K. A. "Quality in Distance Education." *ERIC-Higher Education (ERIC-HE) Digest Series.* EDO-HE-2002–09, 2002a.

Meyer, K. A. *Quality in Distance Education: Focus on Online Learning.* ASHE-ERIC Higher Education Report, vol. 29, no 4. San Francisco: Jossey-Bass, 2002b.

Obler, S., Gabriner, R. S., and Slark, J. "Findings from the California Community College Flashlight Project, 1998–99." Paper presented at the Annual Meeting of the Research and Planning Group for California Community Colleges in Pacific Grove, CA, April 26–28, 2000. (ED 458 916)

Pennsylvania State University. "Emerging Set of Guiding Principles and Practices for the Design and Development of Distance Education." *Innovations in Distance Education.* University Park: Pennsylvania State University, 1998. http://www.cde.psu.edu/DE/IDE/guiding_principles. Accessed Feb. 10, 2004.

Phipps, R. A., and Merisotis, J. P. *What's the Difference? A Review of Contemporary Research on the Effectiveness of Distance Learning in Higher Education.* Washington, D.C.: American Federation of Teachers and National Education Association, 1999.

Phipps, R. A., and Merisotis, J. P. *On the Line: Benchmarks for Success in Internet-Based Distance Education*. Washington, D.C.: The Institute for Higher Education Policy, 2002.

Russell, T. L. *The No Significant Difference Phenomenon*. Raleigh: North Carolina State University, 1999.

Salmon, G. *E-tivities: The Key to Active Online Learning*. London: Kogan Page, 2002.

Shavelson, R. J., and Huang, L. "Responding Responsibly to the Frenzy to Assess Learning in Higher Education." *Change*, 2003, January/February, 11–19.

Southern Association of Colleges and Schools. *Distance Education: Definition and Principles*. Decatur, Ga.: Southern Association of Colleges and Schools, Commission on Colleges, 2001.

Sullivan, P. *Assessing the Impact of Different Modes of Interaction on Student Learning*. Manchester, Conn.: Manchester Community College, 2003.

Terkla, D. T. "Competencies, Regional Accreditation, and Distance Education: An Evolving Role?" In R. A. Voorhees (ed.), *Measuring What Matters: Competency-Based Learning Models in Higher Education*. San Francisco: Jossey-Bass, 2001.

Testa, A., and Bedard-Voorhees, A. "Assessment at Western Governors University." Presentation at the American Association of Higher Education (AAHE) Assessment Conference, Denver, June 1999.

Thach, L., and Murphy, K. L. "Collaboration in Distance Education: From Local to International Perspectives." In L. Foster, B. L. Bower, and L. W. Watson (eds.), *ASHE Reader: Distance Education: Teaching and Learning in Higher Education*. Boston: Pearson, 2002.

Twigg, C. (ed.). *Innovations in Online Learning: Moving Beyond No Significant Difference*. Troy, N.Y.: Center for Academic Transformation, Rensselaer Polytechnic Institute, 2001.

Twigg, C. *Improving Learning and Reducing Costs: Lessons Learned from Round I of the Pew Grant Program in Course Redesign*. Troy, N.Y.: Center for Academic Transformation, Rensselaer Polytechnic Institute, 2003.

Voorhees, R. A. "Feeding Networks: Institutional Research and Uncertainty." Keynote address at the Annual Forum of the Association for Institutional Research, Tampa, Fla., May 2003.

Waits, T., and Lewis, L. "Distance Education and Degree-Granting Postsecondary Education Institutions." NCES 2003–017. Washington, D.C.: U.S. Department of Education, National Center for Education Statistics, 2003.

Western Cooperative for Educational Telecommunications. "Best Practices for Electronically Offered Degree and Certificate Programs." In L. Foster, B. L. Bower, and L. W. Watson (eds.), *ASHE Reader: Distance Education: Teaching and Learning in Higher Education*. Boston: Pearson, 2002.

JOHN MILAM is managing director of HigherEd.org, Inc., in Winchester, Virginia.

RICHARD A. VOORHEES is principal of the Voorhees Group, in Littleton, Colorado.

ALICE BEDARD-VOORHEES is chair for Arts and Humanities, Colorado Community Colleges Online in Denver, Colorado.

8

This chapter provides an overview of the League for Innovation in the Community College's project on learning outcomes. The 21st Century Learning Outcomes Project was a three-year project involving sixteen diverse community colleges that supported the development of practices for assessing and using student learning outcomes to improve student success.

Learning Outcomes for the Twenty-First Century: Cultivating Student Success for College and the Knowledge Economy

Cindy L. Miles, Cynthia Wilson

During the 1990s, community colleges faced mounting external pressure to demonstrate results for what happens in college classrooms and to ensure that their graduates possessed core competencies for success in the burgeoning knowledge economy. McClenney (1998) describes some causes underlying these demands for demonstration of learning outcomes: "The ugly truth about the current situation in American higher education, even in most community colleges, is that we do not a have a clue what and how much students are learning—that is, whether they know and can do what their degree (or other credential) implies" (p. 4).

In summer 2000, with funding from The Pew Charitable Trusts, the League for Innovation in the Community College (the League) developed a network of sixteen pioneering community and technical colleges in the 21st Century Learning Outcomes Project to design and test innovative, outcomes-based methods for defining, delivering, assessing, and documenting student learning. The colleges that participated in the project are Butler County Community College (KS), Central Piedmont Community College (NC), Cuyahoga Community College (OH), Foothill College (CA), Hocking College (OH), Inver Hills Community College (MN), Johnson County Community College (KS), Kingsborough Community College (NY), Mesa Community College (AZ), Midlands Technical College (SC), Montgomery College (TX), San Diego Miramar College (CA), Santa Fe

NEW DIRECTIONS FOR COMMUNITY COLLEGES, no. 126, Summer 2004 © Wiley Periodicals, Inc.

Community College (FL), Schoolcraft College (MI), Skagit Valley College (WA), and Waukesha County Technical College (WI).

The 21st Century Learning Outcomes Project described in this chapter was Stage Two (Implementation and Advocacy) of a larger-scale League effort to bring new outcomes-based standards for student learning to the community college field. In Stage One (Planning and Research), the League, supported by The Pew Charitable Trusts, researched the extent of U.S. and Canadian community college efforts to define, assess, and document student achievement of twenty-first century learning outcomes (Wilson and others, 2000). Stage Two was a three-year project funded for the first two years by The Pew Charitable Trusts and continued with support from the League and participating colleges through June 2003.

The sixteen participating colleges shared a commitment to the project's central goal to increase the capacity of community colleges to define and document the acquisition of the critical competencies that students need to succeed in the workplace, in transfer education, and in today's society. All sixteen colleges developed learning outcomes Web sites to share their project plans, reports, and activities as well as self-assessments, outcomes rubrics, and assessment or documentation models. Many of the colleges are maintaining these public Web sites, accessible through links from the 21st Century Learning Outcomes Project section of the League's Web site (see http://www.league.org/projects/pew).

Approaches to Implementing Learning Outcomes

Over the three years of the 21st Century Learning Outcomes Project, the sixteen participating colleges made individual progress toward the project's goal of enhancing the capacity of community colleges to define and document students' acquisition of critical learning outcomes. Each college worked independently, with feedback and support from partner colleges and project staff, toward the common project goal by focusing on five institutional objectives:

Define. Define a set of core competencies that encompass 21st century learning outcomes.

Develop. Develop a set of curriculum components for 21st century learning outcomes with specific learning outcomes for each competency, levels of performance that students should meet, concrete indices of student work to demonstrate each level, and assessment strategies for measuring student achievement at each level.

Deliver. Identify and implement best practices and multiple models of delivery and assessment of 21st century learning outcomes.

Document. Develop nontraditional methods for documenting student achievement of 21st century learning outcomes beyond traditional grades, credits, and degrees.

Disseminate. Share model programs and practices with other institutions.

The sixteen project colleges came to this work with varying expertise, needs, resources, and constraints regarding student learning outcomes, and college progress toward project objectives varied accordingly. Preliminary focus groups with college leaders in Phase I of the project convinced the funding agency and project directors that community colleges varied too much in structure, governance, and culture to expect a single common solution to such a complex endeavor. Differences notwithstanding, the project partnerships and interchanges led to similarities in outcome sets and in assessment and documentation strategies. Notably, the colleges continue targeted institutional work in support of the project's goal more than a year after the end of the funded phase of the project. Universally, colleges reported achievements in their learning outcomes initiatives, and many point to this project as a landmark in their work toward improving the quality and documentation of student learning in their institutions.

Definition of Learning Outcomes

All sixteen participating colleges successfully identified sets of 21st century learning outcomes for their institutions. The paths that project colleges took to reach these ends varied considerably, as did the resulting sets of learning outcomes, which range in number from four broad knowledge, skill, and ability domains to twenty-seven specific learning competencies. Although only the first step on the learning outcomes journey, reaching shared institutional agreement on the core competencies all those completing degrees or certificates should achieve was a significant undertaking for several colleges, marked by activities spanning a year or more. College approaches to defining student learning outcomes (or critical life skills, essential skills, or core competencies, as they are variously termed), fell into three categories: adoption of the set of "21st century skills," revalidation or amendment of existing sets of competencies associated with the general education core, and development of altogether new sets of core competencies.

Adoption of the Stage One Set of "21st Century Skills." In November 1999, the League convened academic leaders from fifteen colleges to develop consensus on a set of cross-curricular core competencies that two-year college graduates should possess to succeed in work, transfer education, and life. Drawing on results from a preliminary survey and document analysis conducted by League staff, the focus group identified a set of eight broad categories of 21st century skills, encompassing the following so-called hard skills of literacy, numeracy, and technical ability, as well as soft skills such as teamwork, communication, problem solving, and the ability to interact with diverse groups:

- Communication skills (reading, writing, speaking, listening)
- Computation skills (understanding and applying mathematical concepts and reasoning, analyzing and using numerical data)

- Community skills (citizenship; appreciation of diversity and pluralism; local, community, global, and environmental awareness)
- Critical thinking and problem-solving skills (analysis, synthesis, evaluation, decision making, creative thinking)
- Information management skills (collecting, analyzing, and organizing information from a variety of sources)
- Interpersonal skills (teamwork, relationship management, conflict resolution, workplace skills)
- Personal skills (ability to understand and manage self, management of change, learning to learn, personal responsibility, aesthetic responsiveness, wellness)
- Technology skills (computer literacy, Internet skills, retrieving and managing information via technology)

Using these results, the League conducted five institutional site visits and a survey of U.S. and Canadian community colleges to test agreement on this set of 21st century skills and to assess the status of North American community colleges in establishing and assessing student achievement of such skills. Of the 259 institutions that responded to the survey, 92 percent indicated their colleges were addressing the issue of 21st century skills; more than two-thirds identified the 21st century skills from the focus group among their college's list of core competencies, with the exception of personal skills (47 percent) and community skills (59 percent). Two Learning Outcomes Project colleges (Central Piedmont Community College and Santa Fe Community College) adopted the Stage One set of 21st century skills for implementation in their college learning outcomes plan. (For complete Stage One study results see Wilson and others, 2000.)

Revalidation or Amendment of Existing Sets of Core Competencies. Most of the participating colleges (Cuyahoga Community College, Hocking College, Inver Hills Community College, Johnson County Community College, Mesa Community College, Midlands Technical College, Montgomery College, Schoolcraft College, Skagit Valley College, and Waukesha County Technical College) had previously identified sets of core competencies associated with their general education cores. Some of these colleges used project activities to refine their existing competencies, while others with recently developed sets of competencies or more mature learning outcomes approaches moved directly to other project objectives.

A variety of factors, including institutional culture, age of the existing competencies, and workforce demands led colleges on different paths to revising their student learning outcomes. For example, Cuyahoga Community College revalidated its existing General Education and Life Competencies: communication, mathematics, sciences, arts and humanities, social and behavioral sciences, cultural diversity-interdependence-global awareness, computer and information literacy, critical thinking, and consumer awareness and health. As part of its ReVISIONing Learning

Project, Hocking College revalidated its Institutional Core Competencies and renamed them Success Skills to reflect a stronger focus on employer and student learning needs.

Midlands Technical College revised its General Education Core, in place with modifications since 1990, to include an across-the-curriculum emphasis on information literacy, speaking, writing, and teamwork. Skagit Valley College built on general education principles formulated in the early 1990s to create an updated set of learning outcomes for the college, adding principles of technology and management to reflect the skills and knowledge necessary for current academic and workplace success of its students.

Several colleges entered the project with well-developed learning outcomes. Mesa Community College had a mature Student Outcomes Assessment Program, including learning outcomes for general education, the workplace, and developmental education (for a description of the program and assessment results see http://www.mc.maricopa.edu/organizations/employee/orp/assessment). Both Inver Hills Community College and Waukesha County Technical College had fully developed sets of 21st century learning outcomes with extensive rubrics or matrices illustrating levels of student achievement (see Iver Hills' Essential Skills and Rubrics at http://depts.iverhills.edu/LSPS/index.htm and Waukesha's Critical Life Skills Assessment Rubrics at http://www.waukesha.tec.wi.us/home/info/adm/skills.htm).

Through the project, Johnson County Community College (JCCC) built on its nationally recognized Institutional Portfolio model of Institutional Effectiveness evaluation of General Education Learning Outcomes (writing, speaking, culture and ethics, mathematics, modes of inquiry, and problem solving). To review the validity of their general education outcomes, JCCC conducted a 2002 survey with follow-up focus groups of Kansas City business representatives to investigate what skills and abilities employers sought in hiring new workers (Lindahl, 2002). Listening headed the list of sought-after skills in the survey results, followed by personal responsibility and ethics; workplace responsibility, teamwork, and leadership; reading; decision making; observation; and ability to manage self. JCCC has used these findings to strengthen its Keeping Options Open high school career development and academic readiness program (Lindahl, 2002) and to guide development of an outcomes-based curriculum developed in collaboration with area employers and focused on core competencies employees need to be successful (Carlsen, 2002).

Montgomery College demonstrated an unusual approach to building institutional commitment to a core competencies curriculum. Prior to this project, districtwide curriculum teams from the North Harris Montgomery Community College District identified nineteen core competencies to be addressed in all AA or AS degree programs. Still, the Montgomery College Learning Outcomes Team, directed by the college president, invited faculty, administrators, and staff to prepare white papers on each of the eight Stage

One 21st century skills as a way of encouraging broader participation in curriculum reform efforts and to "discern the many nuances of classroom activities that address the core skills at Montgomery College" (Montgomery College, 2004). Volunteer authors included full- and part-time faculty members, associate and assistant deans, and a writing tutor. These papers became a springboard for collegewide electronic dialogues using the Daedalus software system, breakout sessions at the college's annual staff development day, and curriculum renewal efforts in the college's re-accreditation process.

Development of New Sets of Core Competencies. Four colleges (Butler County Community College, Foothill College, Kingsborough Community College, San Diego Miramar College) developed new sets of learning outcomes, giving particular consideration to institutional history or culture that might influence the acceptance and successful implementation of an outcomes-based approach to student learning.

Butler County Community College (BCCC) took a comprehensive, institutional approach to involvement in the Learning Outcomes Project. BCCC's Learning Outcomes Project Team included active involvement from the president; vice president of instruction; chief information officer; dean of business, technology, and workforce development; director of research and institutional effectiveness; director of academic assessment; and director of advising, as well as six faculty members. The team began meeting in November 2000 to make plans for a new, student-centered, faculty-driven program to address learning outcomes. In early 2001, the college determined that its current academic assessment outcomes were inadequate for a program of individualized student assessment and revamped the complex list of Lifetime Learning Abilities and Skills and Performance Characteristics from its earlier learning outcomes plan to a streamlined Learning PACT skills (personal development, analytical, critical thinking, and technological skills). The new Learning PACT outcomes, a set of learning outcomes deemed critical to a person's success in the twenty-first century workplace, were approved by the college's Board of Trustees, and an introduction to the Learning PACT was added to the college Web site and catalogue; distributed in a brochure given to faculty, staff, and students; and included in spring and fall semester college in-service activities (Butler, 2001).

Kingsborough Community College (KCC) also used a strategic institutional approach to identifying learning outcomes that began with a review of the college mission and development of a college values statement. From this foundation, the KCC project team drafted a set of core learning outcomes, shared these with faculty during an open forum and by e-mail for discussion and feedback, and integrated this feedback into a set of learning outcomes comprising seven skill areas: communication (written and oral); critical thinking and problem solving; computation, mathematics, and statistics; interpersonal (teamwork and team building); proficiency in computers and related areas; general education core (science, history, art, and music); and additional knowledge and skills in the major. In keeping with its institutional culture and governance marked by a strong faculty union, KCC reinforced the voluntary nature of participation in its learning outcomes program to encourage grassroots support.

Curriculum Development and Mapping

Participating colleges moved from identification of the critical learning outcomes to be achieved by students to development of comprehensive curriculum components for each outcome with the following elements: levels of performance, concrete indices of student achievement for each level, and assessment strategies for measuring student achievement at each level.

Such curriculum components took shape through the development of extensive learning outcomes rubrics and matrices. The most advanced among the project colleges in learning outcomes curriculum integration, Waukesha County Technical College, has worked since 1986 in a faculty-led grassroots approach to identify and integrate "critical life skills" throughout the curriculum. This integration of skills also extends beyond the classroom to include co-curricular areas such as financial aid, student life, and cooperative education. Waukesha's twenty-three critical life skills are grouped into the four broad areas of communication skills, analytical skills, group effectiveness skills, and personal management skills, with each individual skill defined by a rubric with six levels of indices of student achievement linked to recommended assessments for measuring the achievement of each skill at each level. In addition, each student has a Student Growth and Development Plan that includes a student self-assessment inventory for each of the twenty-three skills as well as a list of suggested services, activities, and programs available to enhance development of each skill. For example, a student assessed as needing development in problem solving is recommended, among other activities, to attend a District Board meeting and observe the decision-making process in action.

Several project colleges have engaged in extensive *curriculum mapping* using the rubrics to determine what courses address which core learning outcomes at what level. As noted, many participating colleges have posted learning outcomes curriculum rubrics and resulting curriculum matrices developed during this project on their public project Web sites.

Implementation

The ultimate goal for *all* project colleges was to implement *all* learning outcomes across the curriculum for *all* students. Colleges decided on one of three areas for initially integrating the outcomes-based curriculum components they developed: in discrete courses, in some programs or academic areas, or across the curriculum. The approaches described below indicate differences only in starting points—that is, how colleges staged their learning outcomes implementation strategies. Within the three years of project activities, colleges moved from discrete course implementation to broader program area implementation for one or more of the learning outcomes. Several moved from pilot courses to programs to integration of one or more learning outcomes across the curriculum.

Implementation in Discrete Courses. A number of colleges began integrating learning outcomes with pilot implementation in a small number of courses. In this approach, a specific course is designed to address one or more learning outcomes (such as writing and critical thinking in a humanities course, computation and problem solving in a math course, diversity awareness in a sociology course), and individual student achievement of learning outcomes is assessed at the individual course level. At Butler County Community College, a speech class and an addictions counseling class pioneered implementing learning outcomes; two years later student learning outcomes are addressed in every course outline and assessed in general education courses across the curriculum.

Implementation in Some Programs or Disciplines. Approaches to curriculum integration at the program level followed three general typologies:

Some courses in some programs are designed to address some learning outcomes; student outcomes achievement is assessed at the course and program levels.

Some programs are designed to address all learning outcomes; student achievement of learning outcomes is assessed at course and program levels.

Certain broad academic areas (such as liberal arts, professional or technical studies) are designed to address all learning outcomes; student outcomes achievement is assessed at the course level.

Several colleges began integration of learning outcomes curriculum approaches across one or two divisions or program areas. At Foothill College, implementation began in fall 2001 in the Computers, Technology, and Information Systems division and the Language Arts division. Since then, the college has developed online course- and program-level matrices for evaluating core competencies across the curriculum. Skagit Valley College updated all its existing program level assessment plans to include 21st century learning outcomes.

Learning Outcomes Implementation Across the Curriculum. Learning outcomes integration across the curriculum followed three general approaches:

One or more learning outcomes are piloted across the curriculum.

Every course is designed to address some number of core competencies (but perhaps not *all* competencies in *all* courses); individual student achievement of learning outcomes is assessed and documented at the course level.

Individual student achievement of learning outcomes is assessed and documented at the program or institutional level.

Hocking College developed a core competency map for each discipline to determine the integration of its success skills. Beginning with the success skill "communicates effectively," each academic program developed its own curriculum map and assessment strategies, such as capstone experiences and the use of internal as well as external evaluators. Similarly, Santa Fe Community College developed a system of curriculum mapping via a learning outcomes audit of all courses to determine the level and indices of each core competency delivered in each course across the curriculum.

At San Diego Miramar College, learning outcomes were integrated into the college's 2000 to 2005 strategic plan, reflecting a shift from broad institutional performance measures toward a focus on individual student learning. Like Foothill College, Miramar developed and implemented online matrix forms to evaluate core competencies at the course and program levels. Through participation in this project, Miramar has developed a comprehensive three-stage approach, with associated instruments, to assess courses and programs for learning outcomes competencies:

Evaluate individual courses (Comprehensive Core Competency Description, Levels of Competency Mastery, Course Assessment Sheet).
Evaluate entire programs (Program Review Assessment Excel Worksheet).
Make necessary changes to course or program content to achieve desired level of learning outcome competency integration.

For a number of years, Mesa Community College (MCC) has been a leader in the outcomes-based education movement and recognized nationally for its collegewide annual student outcomes assessment model. The program is overseen by the Student Outcomes Committee, a standing committee of the Faculty Senate, in collaboration with the dean of instruction. Through its student outcomes assessment program, MCC measures and documents the degree to which a focused sample of students attains specific learning outcomes valued and defined by faculty. MCC's program includes three targeted assessment areas: general education, career and technical education, and developmental education. During its annual Assessment Week, a sample of students participates in assessment of learning outcomes to help answer the question, "Are students learning as a result of their experience at the college?" Assessment results are aggregated and used to measure and compare learning among entering and exiting students. Assessment week results are not made available to individual students; however, results are reported to faculty to guide modification of curriculum and teaching practices. As a result of involvement in this project, Mesa has expanded its assessment pool tenfold to include more than three thousand students from nearly two hundred class sections each year.

A proven leader in implementation of individual student learning outcomes assessment, Waukesha County Technical College (WCTC) has integrated learning outcomes extensively throughout the college curriculum. WCTC has developed comprehensive curriculum rubrics and matrices for each learning outcome, with a plan to make them available electronically to all faculty members for all courses. Through the rubrics and matrices, each learning outcome is plotted throughout a program, indicating the level of its inclusion in a course and the level to which a student must achieve the outcome. Waukesha's Critical Life Skills Assessment Rubrics are available online at http://www.waukesha.tec.wi.us/home/info/adm/skills.htm.

Nontraditional Documentation of Student Learning Outcomes

Several colleges have made advances in nontraditional methods for documenting student achievement of learning outcomes that extend beyond traditional grades, credits, certificates, and degrees, such as electronic transcripts and portfolios (e-transcripts and e-portfolios). In November 2001, Learning Outcomes Project staff conducted an invitational E-Transcript Summit to link project work on nontraditional learning outcomes documentation with similar work in other higher education organizations, including Alverno College, Florida State University, Johns Hopkins University, iLearning Inc., and The Chauncey Group International. Five e-transcript or e-portfolio models were featured: Diagnostic Digital Portfolio, Alverno College; Skills Profile, Inver Hills Community College; Career Portfolio, Florida State University and Santa Fe Community College; Critical Life Skills Transcript, Waukesha County Technical College; and Career Transcript, the Johns Hopkins University. Fifty-eight participants shared best practices and lessons learned from their approaches to electronic documentation, and linkages were made that bolstered documentation activities in project colleges.

Waukesha County Technical College remains involved in implementing its Critical Life Skills electronic transcript, which enables students to demonstrate their growth and development for technical skills and life skills. The transcript includes numerical ratings and descriptions that translate academic language into more commonly understood evidence of student learning. Waukesha also documents learning outcomes in extracurricular activities as well as in traditional courses.

Inver Hills Community College designed an Internet-deployed database to record and report student achievement. Faculty apply cross-disciplinary rubrics defining exemplary, acceptable, and unacceptable achievement levels to assignments, tests, and projects. (See http://depts. inverhills.edu/LSPS.rubrics.htm for the rubrics and a sample Skills Profile.) Students then receive a Skills Profile—a complement to the traditional transcript—that documents their skills, citing specific projects, tests, or assignments as evidence. In the early phases of the Internet system, a small group of volunteer faculty participated; however, faculty members now use the

Internet to track levels of achievement for each competency, and the project is stimulating faculty involvement toward a goal of institutionalizing this approach to documentation of learning outcomes. Currently, e-transcripts and e-portfolios documenting student learning outcomes are under development or implementation at six of the project colleges: Waukesha County Technical College, Inver Hills Community College, Schoolcraft College, Johnson County Community College, Hocking College, and Midlands Technical College.

Unexpected Outcomes

Although the project began with the goal of cultivating a focus on learning outcomes, several college teams quickly found this work to be a catalyst for major institutional change. In some cases, it led to a complete shift in approach, particularly for colleges that had extensive institutional effectiveness and program review processes but no comprehensive processes for assessing and documenting learning at the individual student level. For others, the project served as a means of connecting a number of loosely related initiatives all aimed at improving the quality of undergraduate education.

Shifts in thinking occurred in curriculum design, with an emphasis on learning outcomes replacing a traditional focus on course objectives. Colleges also began exploring ways of ensuring that student learning outcomes would become the central success factors used in determining institutional effectiveness.

Why Is This So Hard?

Throughout the project, the recurring refrain was the same: "This is hard work!" McClenney (2001), the project's external evaluator, identified key reasons that colleges find this undertaking so difficult:

- Lack of collaboration among disciplines and other groups within the institution
- Lack of knowledge about assessment processes and tools
- Lack of awareness of the need for outcomes-based education
- Lack of appropriate, effective assessment tools and models
- A perception that some important learning outcomes are not measurable
- Traditional insulation from accountability for individual student learning at the classroom level
- Traditional resistance to self-assessment in higher education
- Lack of incentive for outcomes-based efforts resulting from past external requirements for accountability, funding, and policy that are rarely tied to individual student learning
- Increasing demands and constricting resources, which leave little time or incentive for educational reform efforts of this magnitude

Assessment Is the Really Hard Part

Throughout the project, participants universally identified assessment as the most difficult aspect of this work, and during seminars, focus groups, and site visits they explored the reasons for this determination. Team members from all areas of the colleges admitted that they do not know how to assess and that, as one participant put it, "the tools stink." One participant explained the difficulty with assessing learning outcomes by pointing out, "We are unaccustomed to being asked to gain consensus on what we're trying to achieve." Another acknowledged the bliss of ignorance as a complement to the fear of failure, noting, "We don't really want to know how we measure up." The lack of data also makes the work more difficult. As one member put it, "We don't know what we don't know." And still another pointed to the busy schedules of everyone in the college: "I'm already dancing as fast as I can." Despite these challenges, most college team members agreed that the hard work was worth it, citing such advantages as "Faculty and students are completely transformed in their thinking about why they are here," and "For the first time we can begin to answer the 'How do we know?' questions about learning."

Recommendations

Nearly all of the sixteen colleges that joined the 21st Century Learning Outcomes Project with the League in July 2000 remain engaged more than three years later in targeted institutional work toward implementing their learning outcomes agendas. Today many others have joined these colleges as the learning outcomes movement gains momentum in higher education, with accrediting commissions and other higher education associations advancing the cause. Other institutions embarking on a learning outcomes journey might take the following lessons from the pioneering experiences of these sixteen forerunners:

Learning outcomes implementation must be a continuous campus conversation. Such conversation allows for more natural emergence and implementation of ideas and integrates new employees into the ongoing conversation with veteran staff, through which they learn the history of the process, participate in the current analysis and implementation, and help shape the future through continued discussion.

The impetus for adopting an outcomes-based approach should be the institution's stated and lived value of student learning. Colleges may adopt an outcomes-based approach to learning as a means of pacifying external demands for accountability or securing sufficient funding; however, if the motivation for change does not stem from an explicit focus on student learning, the effort may fall short of its potential.

Since the accountability movement is not progressing in some colleges with the speed and urgency it might if the need were critical, other motivators can be effective. The movement to an outcomes-based educational approach can be adopted, for example, as a means of clearly distinguishing an institution in a crowded, competitive market. The movement may be prompted by the vision of a strong leader or the experience and prestige that come from joining a cutting-edge movement.

Faculty should be deeply engaged and supported from the onset in the leadership of any effort toward outcomes-based learning. Full support of faculty should include adequate professional development and reassigned workload for new curriculum development. Special assistance should be provided as needed, particularly from experts in outcomes-based curriculum and assessment when redesigning curriculum. Taking the stance that this is work that faculty should be doing anyway is likely to be counterproductive; instead, acknowledging the outstanding work faculty are already doing and finding incentives to help them shift traditional teaching and curriculum methods to more outcomes-based approaches will be more successful.

A college should implement outcomes-based learning using a model that fits its culture and values. In no case should a college adopt another institution's program wholesale; however, a college can customize one or more approaches that resonate with its fundamental philosophy. Learning outcomes approaches and assessment of student learning can strengthen academic quality and institutional effectiveness (Baker and Hjelm, 2001).

Clearly, one of the major lessons of this project is that this work is extremely difficult. Changing a college culture to a focus on learning outcomes requires long-term commitment and dedication of resources. Internal as well as external forces can cause the work to ebb and flow.

Although cuts in budget, changes in leadership, and temporary shifts in priorities pull colleges from this work, the underlying commitment to student learning remains. What matters most is that a learning outcomes approach can help a college demonstrate to its students that it offers them relevant curricula, meaningful information about their learning achievements, and more control over their learning to help them prepare for success in their professional and personal lives.

References

Baker, R. L., and Hjelm, M. "Evaluating Individual Student Learning: Implications from Four Models of Assessment." *Learning Abstracts,* 2001, 4(3).

Butler County Community College. Learning PACT Project: Quarterly Report, October 2001. http://www.butlercc.edu/league. Accessed Jan. 31, 2004.

Carlsen, C. J., "Leading the Way to Connect Community to the College." *Leadership Abstracts,* 2002, 15(9).

Lindahl, S. "Learning Options and Readiness: High School Partnerships in the 21st Century." *Learning Abstracts,* 2002, 5(2).

McClenney, K. M. "Community Colleges Perched at the Millennium: Perspectives on Innovation, Transformation, and Tomorrow." *Leadership Abstracts,* 1998, 11(8).

McClenney, K. M. "Why Is This So Hard. . . . And Why Bother?" 21st Century Learning Outcomes Project Seminar 2001. League for Innovation in the Community College. March 4, 2001, Atlanta.

Montgomery College. *21st Century Learning Outcomes Project: White Papers.* http://www.woodstock.edu/students/academics/learningoutcomes/index.html. Accessed Jan. 31, 2004.

Wilson, C. D., Miles, C. L., Baker, R. L., and Schoenberger, R. L. *Learning Outcomes for the 21st Century: Report of a Community College Study.* Mission Viejo, Calif.: League for Innovation in the Community College, 2000.

CINDY L. MILES *is vice president for learning and academic affairs at Community College of Denver and senior consultant with the League for Innovation in the Community College.*

CYNTHIA WILSON *is vice president for learning and research at the League for Innovation in the Community College. Cindy and Cynthia co-directed the League's 21st Century Learning Outcomes Project.*

9

Although community colleges have made significant strides in assessing student learning outcomes, there are a number of significant challenges that need to be addressed in order to realize fully the anticipated benefits of these efforts. This chapter identifies these major challenges and provides specific suggestions that can be used by community colleges, state and accrediting agencies, and universities to facilitate the development, implementation, and continued support of student learning outcomes assessment initiatives that will increase student learning and achievement.

Meeting the Challenges of Assessing Student Learning Outcomes

Jack Friedlander, Andreea M. Serban

Why are so many community colleges finding it so difficult to design, develop, implement, and sustain a comprehensive approach to assessing student learning outcomes? Why do community college practitioners need to devote so much time at their individual campuses trying to discover how to approach assessing student learning outcomes? More specifically, why are community colleges each being asked to start from scratch in figuring out how to assess student learning outcomes? Why is there so little evidence that multi-year efforts to assess student learning outcomes affect student learning and development and the achievement of desired institutional outcomes?

This chapter has three purposes: to identify the primary challenges community colleges need to address in developing, implementing, and sustaining a comprehensive approach to assessing student learning outcomes; to offer suggestions for how community college practitioners can respond to each of these challenges; and to advance recommendations for providing colleges with the technical assistance they need to implement and sustain a comprehensive approach to assessing student learning outcomes that will achieve the desired learning, improvement, and accountability outcomes of assessment.

Primary Challenges and Recommendations

Based on our review of the literature, including the chapters contained in this issue and conversations with practitioners and leaders involved in assessing student learning outcomes, we have identified four major challenges that need to be addressed if the desired goals for assessing student

NEW DIRECTIONS FOR COMMUNITY COLLEGES, no. 126, Summer 2004 © Wiley Periodicals, Inc.

learning outcomes are to be fully achieved. A number of recommendations targeted to specific constituencies are offered to address each of the challenges identified.

First Challenge. There is a lack of evidence that multi-year efforts to assess student learning outcomes affect student learning and development, achievement of desired institutional outcomes, instructional methods, co-curricular programs, and college policies and processes. The observations and conclusions made by several of the authors in this volume offer insights on why full models for assessing student learning outcomes that practitioners could adapt for their own institutions are not available. In Chapter Seven, Milam, Voorhees, and Bedard-Voorhees state, "Regional accreditors describe their expectations for measuring learning outcomes differently. . . . Most standards suggested by the regional accrediting agencies generally encompass what should be required of colleges, but there is little guidance how to measure competencies or units of learning they imply or even what those competencies are. It is ironic that regional accreditors suggest that colleges produce favorable assessment results when the knowledge base that might drive such accreditation decisions, especially the measurement of student learning, has not been fully informed by practice."

In Chapter One, Banta, Black, Kahn, and Jackson talk about the importance of providing stakeholders with credible evidence on the benefits of assessing student learning outcomes in improving and sustaining assessment. They observe, "Unfortunately, credible evidence of learning and effectiveness can be elusive. . . . To date, however, community colleges and their stakeholders have not resolved what constitutes credible evidence in all areas of their mission."

In his comprehensive analysis of the status of student learning assessment, Volkwein (2003) noted, "Faculty are most enthusiastic about assessment when they fully understand what assessment is and how they and their students can benefit. When assessment is focused on improving teaching and learning, faculty recognize it as being connected to their interests" (p. 9). However, Volkwein goes on to state that knowledge of the effects of the use of assessment in higher education on student performance, instructional methods, and academic policy remains limited.

In Chapter Four, Bers examines program-level assessment in community colleges (other than those in English composition, mathematics, or from programs other than those in health careers or with certification or license exams). She was not able to find many examples of program-level assessment that are actually being done rather than planned, or assessments that have generated results then used for improving or sustaining program quality. She concluded that program-level assessment at community colleges is still in its infancy.

Although much has been written about the importance of linking the assessment of outcomes to improvement of student learning and development, there has been limited documentation of how the assessment results have been used to guide instructional methods. Other than examples of classroom assessment techniques used to assess specific aspects of student learning, such as those described in Chapter Three, there is an absence of literature linking various pedagogical techniques to the promotion of the desired student learning outcomes. The assessment processes used by colleges are often silent on the training required in the area of pedagogy, instructional methods, and co-curricular programs that promote student attainment of desired learning outcomes. Similarly, little or no attention has been given to changes in institutional policies and procedures to support the assessment effort (for example, faculty evaluation policies and incentives, adequate support services, linking faculty professional development efforts to support student learning outcomes assessment, program definition, and clarification of student expectations and standards).

Recommendations Directed to Community College Practitioners. Authors in Chapters One, Three, and Eight provide excellent examples of the processes for engaging the campus community in the student learning assessment effort. However, colleges need to go beyond processes to identify how best to measure, analyze, interpret, and report the results of this effort. For each student learning outcome to be achieved, whether at the course, program, or institutional level, there has to be a clear definition of the skill (competency) to be acquired; assessment tool(s) or technique(s) used to measure the attainment of the skill; and measurement, documentation, and reporting of the actual extent to which the skill has been acquired.

An overall framework for reporting the achievement of desired student learning outcomes is needed at the course, program, and institutional levels. The framework should allow institutions to compare changes over time, both at the aggregate and granular levels (for example, entry levels of skills for various groups of students).

Colleges must provide professional development opportunities for faculty and co-curricular staff on effective pedagogical techniques and intervention strategies that support the attainment of specific student learning outcomes. For example, few faculty outside English have received any formal training in teaching reading, writing, or public speaking skills. If a desired outcome is to improve students' communication skills (reading, writing, speaking, listening), then faculty teaching outside of the English and Communications departments need to receive training on effective strategies and instructional methods for developing, assessing, and assisting students with these skills. A similar statement could be made for each of the other desired general education skills and competencies discussed in Chapter Eight (such as computation skills, community skills, critical thinking and problem-solving skills, information management skills, interpersonal skills, personal skills, and technology skills).

Recommendations Directed to State and Accrediting Agencies. State and accrediting agencies should provide guidance regarding the core student learning outcomes that should be achieved by community colleges for each of their various missions. The guide would allow for colleges to adopt or adapt the student learning outcomes and align them with their particular environments. These guides should also include suggested methods, tools, instruments for assessing each of the desired student learning outcomes and, if possible, normative data to provide baselines for comparisons.

The suggested core student learning outcomes should go beyond traditional institutional output measures such as course completion rates, number of degrees awarded, number of students transferring, and job placement rates mentioned in Chapter Five.

State and accrediting agencies should identify qualified individuals whom colleges could call upon to assist with student learning outcomes assessment. If possible, these individuals should complete certification training to ensure that colleges will receive appropriate guidance and assistance in their assessment efforts.

These recommendations would save each college an enormous amount of time and resources in determining how to define, collect, analyze, and report student learning outcomes. The need for such assistance is obvious: after more than two decades of attempting to assess student learning outcomes, community college practitioners are still unclear on how to conduct a comprehensive program of assessment of student learning outcomes effectively.

Second Challenge. There is a lack of knowledge about assessment processes, tools, and models. Generally, at any given college, few faculty and staff have been formally trained in developing measurable and valid learning outcomes; aligning the curriculum with those outcomes; developing assessment questions, instruments, and methods; and developing and implementing a plan for assessing those outcomes that is manageable, meaningful, and sustainable. In addition, few colleges have an infrastructure in place to provide the technical knowledge and support to assist full- and part-time faculty with the design, collection, analysis, and application of assessment data. Moreover, few institutions have designated staff member(s) with the time, knowledge, and skills to link course, program, and institutional learning outcomes or to disseminate the results of the student learning outcomes efforts.

Throughout this volume, each of the authors points to the lack of knowledge in this area as a major impediment. For example, in Chapter Eight, Miles and Wilson cite the following observation of their external evaluator: "Participants universally identified assessment as the most difficult aspect of this work. . . . Team members from all areas of the colleges admitted that they do not know how to assess."

Recommendations Directed to Community College Practitioners. Prior to engaging in any institution-wide assessment of student learning outcomes effort, colleges need to develop a comprehensive plan to provide faculty and staff with the competencies they need to conduct assessment. As Serban suggests in Chapter Two, a college could start by identifying individuals on campus with relevant skills who could provide leadership and ongoing technical support for this effort. Since it is unlikely that any one person would have knowledge in all required areas of assessment (including constructing valid test questions, methods of evaluating writing, critical thinking, and an array of assessment techniques such as embedded course assessment, authentic assessment techniques, performance-based outcomes measures, holistic scoring, and portfolio analysis), a team of faculty and staff with in-house expertise would need to be assembled. If appropriate, one or more consultants may need to be employed to assist this team in developing and enhancing its expertise and in crafting a plan for providing ongoing technical support and training for both full- and part-time instructors at the college. Colleges should start with a subset of courses and conduct a pilot study to evaluate all aspects of the assessment process.

Recommendations Directed to State and Accrediting Agencies. States and accrediting agencies should provide training materials on assessment processes, tools, and models that can be used by faculty and staff at individual colleges. In addition to training materials, states and accrediting agencies should sponsor workshops through a variety of delivery modes to assist colleges in using the training materials developed and to disseminate best practices.

Third Challenge. It is difficult to gain consensus among faculty in what they are trying to achieve at the course, program, and college levels. Generally, course outlines include a list of objectives and methods of measuring those objectives. However, these objectives are not necessarily student learning outcomes and are not stated in measurable terms. Also these objectives are typically stated broadly, without specificity in terms of particular skills or competencies that students should acquire. In most community colleges, faculty have not had a tradition of working together at the department level to develop student learning outcomes at a granular level and methods for assessing those outcomes. More specifically, most faculty have not had the training or experience in identifying student learning outcomes and how they should be assessed, or in determining the level of ability or knowledge students should attain to reflect adequate or excellent learning standards.

In Chapter Four, Bers identified the challenges of program assessment at community colleges. These challenges include difficulty in defining a program, the very diverse course-taking patterns of students, and the large percentage of students who take courses at multiple institutions or from colleges within or outside multicampus institutions.

Similar challenges exist at the institutional level. These challenges are compounded by the fact that colleges have no experience or models for how to develop and sustain a comprehensive effort for assessing student learning outcomes at the institutional level.

Recommendations Directed to Community College Practitioners. Faculty need to have an understanding of how student learning outcomes assessment at the course and program levels contributes to institutional goal achievement. As stated earlier, colleges should provide faculty in each department or discipline with the training and technical support required to develop meaningful and measurable student learning outcomes. Colleges need to develop strategies to ensure that the methods identified for assessing student learning outcomes are used consistently by all faculty members, including those teaching part-time, evenings, and in off-campus locations or through alternative instructional methods such as online and distance learning.

Faculty need to have systematic feedback on the extent to which the assessment conducted is making a difference in student learning and providing success at the course, program, and institutional levels. Assessing student learning outcomes should result in a clear identification of skills, competencies, and disposition toward learning with which students need additional assistance.

Faculty should have viable options for providing students with the assistance needed in a timely fashion. One of the options must address how to integrate student support programs and services effectively with the classroom instructional processes.

Recommendations Directed to State and Accrediting Agencies. State agencies and regional community colleges consortia should promote inter-institutional networks of faculty and co-curricular support staff to facilitate sharing of teaching and assessment techniques at both the discipline and institution-wide levels.

States should encourage, if not require, faculty from community colleges and four-year institutions to work jointly in developing standard student learning outcomes for each lower-division course in each major for which articulation agreements exist. Developing common student learning outcomes, methods for assessing the attainment of those outcomes, and standards of achievement should result in stronger articulation of courses and programs, easier student transition from community colleges to transfer institutions, and a greater degree of sharing and collaboration among faculty on best practices in pedagogy and assessment. Similar collaboration is needed in the area of co-curricular programs and services.

States should consider developing curriculum guidelines for remedial, core general education, and occupational education courses for which there is no specialized accreditation or external certification. These curriculum frameworks could include identification of student learning outcomes to be achieved; examples of assessment measures, tests, or other instruments that could be used; and illustrations of effective instructional strategies for promoting the attainment of desired student learning outcomes. Faculty and staff from all segments of education, secondary and post-secondary, should be involved in developing and updating these curriculum frameworks.

Fourth Challenge. Implementing and sustaining a comprehensive student learning outcomes assessment effort in a community college setting is difficult. As previously noted, the processes community colleges can follow to build support for and engage faculty and staff in the development of assessment of student learning outcomes have been well documented. However, as Serban pointed out in Chapter Two, what is missing from the literature are specific models for developing, implementing, and sustaining comprehensive assessment efforts that take into account the particular features of a community college setting. These include multiple and diverse missions; transient student populations with various educational goals and needs, which frequently do not include completing courses, programs, certificates, or degrees in the prescribed sequence; a large cadre of part-time faculty; delivery of instruction and services in multiple locations of an institution; and limited technical staff to support all phases of student learning outcomes assessment.

Beno notes in Chapter Six that accrediting agencies anticipate that it will take colleges ten to fifteen years to implement their student learning outcomes assessment initiatives. A significant challenge facing community colleges is the lack of adequate time, resources, and incentives to engage in an educational reform of this magnitude. This is particularly the case now that colleges have entered once again into an era of scarce resources, when faculty and staff feel overextended, and institutional budgets continue to be constrained if not reduced.

Recommendations Directed to Community College Practitioners. In developing their overall plans for assessment, colleges need to take into consideration the financial and human resources required to support implementing and sustaining such efforts. As previously noted, colleges need to allocate or re-allocate resources to such areas as training, technical support staff, development of information systems needed to capture assessment data, and staff to analyze, report, and disseminate assessment results.

In order to sustain such an effort, colleges need to provide each of their constituencies with evidence that this allocation of scarce resources results in improved student learning and achievement greater than might have been achieved had the resources been applied differently.

Given the magnitude of what colleges are being asked to achieve, coupled with the lack of adequate models, tools, and staff and financial resources to do so, colleges will be well advised to focus their efforts to assess and improve student learning outcomes in a limited number of courses and programs. If successful, they can generalize their approaches to other parts of the curriculum.

Recommendations Directed to State and Accrediting Agencies. As noted by Milam, Voorhees, and Bedard-Voorhees in Chapter Seven, accrediting agencies have spearheaded the drive for institutions to measure student learning outcomes prior to their having evidence that the new requirements will in fact produce the desired results. Furthermore, they are requiring each institution to engage in this transformational effort with limited guidance on what is expected in terms of student learning outcomes to be achieved or effective models and tools for doing so. This has resulted in each institution having to spend far more time and resources than would have been required had the accrediting agencies done appropriate pilot testing and evaluation of the success of their requirements prior to imposing them on all institutions. Since some accrediting agencies have been asking for such evidence for an extended period of time, it is now time for them to step back and evaluate their requirements and to provide community colleges with much greater guidance and assistance than now exists.

State agencies need to define what they expect from community colleges in terms of student learning outcomes assessment. Moreover, there is a lack of connection between what states are requesting for institutional accountability and what accrediting agencies are now requiring of colleges with respect to student learning outcomes assessment. As noted by Burke and Minassians in Chapter Five, to date, states have limited their performance measures to institutional outputs (such as number of degrees, licensure exam rates, number of transfers, enrollment trends, time to degree, and college participation rates) rather than to student learning outcomes. The state measures have not taken into account the multiple missions and diverse clientele of community colleges. Similarly, the states need to identify what resources and incentives they need to provide to sustain the college student learning outcomes assessment efforts.

Conclusion

The chapters in this volume cover many of the critical components of assessment of student learning outcomes. They provide an overview of the issues, methods, and challenges that community colleges face in developing and implementing core components of their student learning outcomes assessment initiatives. In addition, the volume includes many specific examples from colleges across the country of how various components of student learning outcomes assessment have been developed and implemented.

While each of the authors underscored the importance of measuring student learning outcomes, they each noted the formidable challenges colleges face in doing so. The purpose of this chapter was to identify the major challenges that, if not addressed, will continue to serve as barriers to realizing fully the anticipated benefits of requiring colleges to measure student learning outcomes. We have noted that much can be done by state and accrediting agencies, as well as by the colleges themselves, to help overcome these challenges. In addition, universities with graduate programs for higher education should consider offering specialized training for graduate students and practitioners in all aspects of student learning outcomes assessment. Graduate schools should incorporate into their teaching training programs methods for assessing and improving the attainment of student learning outcomes. Researchers in all disciplines need to focus more of their efforts on identifying, evaluating, and disseminating effective strategies for measuring and improving attainment of desired student learning outcomes.

Reference

Volkwein, J. F. "Implementing Outcomes Assessment on Your Campus." *The RP Group eJournal*, *1*, May 2003. http://rpgroup.org/publications/eJournal/Volume_1/volume_1.htm. Accessed Feb. 16, 2004.

JACK FRIEDLANDER is executive vice president for educational programs at Santa Barbara City College in Santa Barbara, California.

ANDREEA M. SERBAN is associate vice president for information resources and director of institutional assessment, research, and planning at Santa Barbara City College in Santa Barbara, California.

INDEX

Holm, A., 3, 29, 42
Huang, L., 74
Hudgins, J., 5
Hutchings, P., 7

Implementing outcomes assessment principles, 9–11
Improving outcomes assessment principles, 11–14
Institutional or departmental testing, 46–47
Institutions: assessment expertise and skills available at, 23–25; developing accreditation culture/practice by, 71–72; difficulty of defining effectiveness indicators, 13; educational purposes, learning objectives, and assessment of, 17–22; increasing support from external stakeholders, 5; practical accreditation guidance for, 68–70; reporting and using assessment results, 22–23; student learning outcomes addressed by, 70–71. *See also* Community colleges; Higher education
Inver Hills Community College (Minnesota), 87, 90, 91, 96, 97
INVEST system, 19

Jackson, J. E., 2, 5, 16, 102
Jamison, T. M., 82
Jansak, K. E., 80
Johnson County Community College (Kansas), 87, 90, 91, 97
Jones, E. A., 78
Jones, K., 9, 13

Kahn, S., 2, 5, 16, 102
Keup, J. R., 18, 19
Kingsborough Community College (South Carolina), 87, 92–93
Kluber, A., 13

Laidig, J., 47
Lane Community College (Oregon), 11, 12–13
League for Innovation in the Community College (the League), 87, 88, 98
Learning communities, 20, 80
Learning outcomes. *See* Student learning outcomes
Learning PACT skills (BCCC), 92
LeGuardia Community College (New York), 50

Lewis, D. R., 25
Lewis, L., 73
Lindahl, S., 91
Lopez, C., 33
Lund, J. P., 7

McClenney, K. M., 5, 87, 97
McKnight, R., 78
Maki, P. L., 67
Maricopa Community College District (Phoenix), 80
Massy, W. F., 5
Measuring Up 2000, 63
Measuring Up 2002, 63
Mee, G., 71
Mellon Foundation, 75
Memory Matrix, 32
Merisotis, J. P., 82
Mesa Community College (Arizona), 70–71, 87, 90, 91, 95
Meyer, K. A., 74
Miami-Dade Community College (Florida), 19
Midlands Technical Community College (South Carolina), 13–14, 87, 90, 91, 97
Milam, J., 3, 73, 85, 102
Miles, C. L., 3, 87, 100
Minassians, H. P., 3, 53, 54, 59, 64, 108
Montgomery College Learning Outcomes Team, 91–92
Montgomery College (Texas), 87, 90
Moore, A., 19, 20
Motivational Systems Theory, 82
Mt. Hood Community College (Oregon), 9
Muddiest Point CAT, 34
Murphy, K. L., 81

Narratives, 47–48
National Center for Education Statistics survey (2000), 18
National Center for Public Policy and Higher Education, 63
National Postsecondary Education Cooperative, 77
National Student Clearinghouse Enrollment Search program, 48
National Survey of Student Engagement, 21
North Harris Montgomery Community College District, 91
Nova Scotia Community College System (Canada), 19

Back Issue/Subscription Order Form

Copy or detach and send to:

Jossey-Bass, A Wiley Imprint, 989 Market Street, San Francisco CA 94103-1741

Call or fax toll-free: Phone 888-378-2537 6:30AM – 3PM PST; Fax 888-481-2665

Back Issues: Please send me the following issues at $29 each
(Important: please include ISBN number with your order.)

_____

_____

_____

$ _____   Total for single issues

$ _____   SHIPPING CHARGES: SURFACE   Domestic Canadian
First Item $5.00 $6.00
Each Add'l Item $3.00 $1.50
For next-day and second-day delivery rates, call the number listed above.

Subscriptions   Please __ start __ renew my subscription to *New Directions for Community Colleges* for the year 2____at the following rate:

U.S.	__ Individual $80	__ Institutional $165
Canada	__ Individual $80	__ Institutional $165
All Others	__ Individual $104	__ Institutional $239
Online Subscription		__ Institutional $165

**For more information about online subscriptions visit
www.interscience.wiley.com**

$ _____   Total single issues and subscriptions (Add appropriate sales tax for your state for single issue orders. No sales tax for U.S. subscriptions. Canadian residents, add GST for subscriptions and single issues.)

__Payment enclosed (U.S. check or money order only)

__VISA __ MC __ AmEx __ # _____Exp. Date _____

Signature _____ Day Phone _____

__ Bill Me (U.S. institutional orders only. Purchase order required.)

Purchase order # _____
Federal Tax ID13559302   GST 89102 8052

Name _____

Address _____

_____

Phone _____   E-mail _____

For more information about Jossey-Bass, visit our Web site at www.josseybass.com

OTHER TITLES AVAILABLE IN THE
NEW DIRECTIONS FOR COMMUNITY COLLEGES SERIES
Arthur M. Cohen, Editor-in-Chief
Florence B. Brawer, Associate Editor

CC125 **Legal Issues in the Community College**
Robert C. Cloud
Community colleges must be prepared for lawsuits, federal statutes, court
rulings, union negotiations, and other legal issues that could affect
institutional stability and effectiveness. This volume provides leaders with
information about board relations, tenure and employment, student rights
and safety, disability law, risk management, copyright and technology issues,
and more.
ISBN: 0-7879-7482-X

CC124 **Successful Approaches to Fundraising and Development**
Mark David Milliron, Gerardo E. de los Santos, Boo Browning
This volume outlines how community colleges can tap into financial support
from the private sector, as four-year institutions have been doing. Chapter
authors discuss building community college foundations, cultivating
relationships with the local community, generating new sources of revenue,
fundraising from alumni, and the roles of boards, presidents, and trustees.
ISBN: 0-7879-7283-5

CC123 **Help Wanted: Preparing Community College Leaders in a New Century**
William E. Piland, David B. Wolf
This issue brings together various thoughtful perspectives on the nature of
leading community colleges over the foreseeable future. Authors offer
suggestions for specific programmatic actions that community colleges
themselves can take to provide the quantity, quality, specializations, and
diversity of leaders that are needed.
ISBN: 0-7879-7248-7

CC122 **Classification Systems for Two-Year Colleges**
Alexander C. McCormick, Rebecca D. Cox
This critically important volume advances the conversation among
researchers and practitioners about possible approaches to classifying two-
year colleges. After an introduction to the history, purpose, practice, and
pitfalls of classifying colleges and universities, five different classification
schemes are presented, followed by commentary by knowledgable
respondents representing potential users of a classification system:
community college associations, institutional leaders, and researchers. The
final chapter applies the five proposed schemes to a sample of colleges for
purposes of illustration.
ISBN: 0-7879-7171-5

CC121 **The Role of the Community College in Teacher Education**
Barbara K. Townsend, Jan M. Ignash
Illustrates the extent to which community colleges have become major
players in teacher education, not only in the traditional way of providing the
first two years of an undergraduate degree in teacher education but in more
controversial ways such as offering associate and baccalaureate degrees in
teacher education and providing alternative certification programs.
ISBN: 0-7879-6868-4

CC120   **Enhancing Community Colleges Through Professional Development**
Gordon E. Watts
Offers a much needed perspective on the expanding role of professional
development in community colleges. Chapter authors provide descriptions
of how their institutions have addressed issues through professional
development, created institutional change, developed new delivery systems
for professional development, reached beyond development just for faculty,
and found new uses for traditional development activities.
ISBN: 0-7879-6330-5

CC119   **Developing Successful Partnerships with Business and the Community**
Mary S. Spangler
Demonstrates that there are many different approaches to community
colleges' partnering with the private sector and that when partners are
actively engaged in tailoring education, training, and learning to their
students, everyone is the beneficiary.
ISBN: 0-7879-6321-9

CC118   **Community College Faculty: Characteristics, Practices, and Challenges**
Charles Outcalt
Offers multiple perspectives on the ways community college faculty fulfill
their complex professional roles. With data from national surveys, this
volume provides an overview of community college faculty, looks at their
primary teaching responsibility, and examines particular groups of
instructors, including part-timers, women, and people of color.
ISBN: 0-7879-6328-3

CC117   **Next Steps for the Community College**
Trudy H. Bers, Harriott D. Calhoun
Provides an overview of relevant literature and practice covering major
community college topics: transfer rates, vocational education, remedial
and developmental education, English as a second language education,
assessment of student learning, student services, faculty and staff, and
governance and policy. Includes a chapter discussing the categories,
types, and purposes of literature about community colleges and the
major publications germane to community college practitioners and
scholars.
ISBN: 0-7879-6289-9

CC116   **The Community College Role in Welfare to Work**
C. David Lisman
Provides examples of effective programs including a job placement program
meeting the needs of rural welfare recipients, short-term and advanced levels
of technical training, a call center program for customer service job training,
beneficial postsecondary training, collaborative programs for long-term
family economic self-sufficiency, and a family-based approach recognizing
the needs of welfare recipients and their families.
ISBN: 0-7879-5781-X

CC115 **The New Vocationalism in Community Colleges**
Debra D. Bragg
Analyzes the role of community college leaders in developing programs, successful partnerships and collaboration with communities, work-based learning, changes in perception of terminal education and transfer education, changing instructional practices for changing student populations and the integration of vocational education into the broader agenda of American higher education.
ISBN: 0-7879-5780-1

CC114 **Transfer Students: Trends and Issues**
Frankie Santos Laanan
Evaluates recent research and policy discussions surrounding transfer students, and summarizes three broad themes in transfer policy: research, student and academic issues, and institutional factors. Argues that institutions are in a strategic position to provide students with programs for rigorous academic training as well as opportunities to participate in formal articulation agreements with senior institutions.
ISBN: 0-7879-5779-8

CC113 **Systems for Offering Concurrent Enrollment at High Schools and Community Colleges**
Piedad F. Robertson, Brian G. Chapman, Fred Gaskin
Offers approaches to creating valuable programs, detailing all the components necessary for the success and credibility of concurrent enrollment. Focuses on the faculty liaisons from appropriate disciplines that provide the framework for an ever-improving program.
ISBN: 0-7879-5758-5

CC112 **Beyond Access: Methods and Models for Increasing Retention and Learning Among Minority Students**
Steven R. Aragon
Presents practical models, alternative approaches and new strategies for creating effective cross-cultural courses that foster higher retention and learning success for minority students. Argues that educational programs must now develop a broader curriculum that includes multicultural and multi-linguistic information.
ISBN: 0-7879-5429-2

CC111 **How Community Colleges Can Create Productive Collaborations with Local Schools**
James C. Palmer
Details ways that community colleges and high schools can work together to help students navigate the difficult passage from secondary to higher education. Provides detailed case studies of actual collaborations between specific community colleges and high school districts, discuss legal problems that can arise when high school students enroll in community colleges, and more.
ISBN: 0-7879-5428-4

CC110   **Building Successful Relationships Between Community Colleges and the
        Media**
        Clifton Truman Daniel, Hanel Henriksen Hastings
        Explores current relationships between two-year colleges and the media
        across the country, reviewing the history of community colleges'
        relationships with members of the press, examining the media's relationships
        with community college practitioners, and offering practical strategies for
        advancing an institution's visibility.
        ISBN: 0-7879-5427-6

CC109   **Dimensions of Managing Academic Affairs in the Community College**
        Douglas Robillard, Jr.
        Offers advice on fulfilling the CAO's academic duties, and explores the
        CAO's faculty and administrative roles, discussing how to balance the
        sometimes conflicting roles of faculty mentor, advocate, and disciplinarian
        and the importance of establishing a synergistic working relationship with
        the president.
        ISBN: 0-7879-5369-5

CC108   **Trends in Community College Curriculum**
        Gwyer Schuyler
        Presents a detailed picture of the national community college curriculum,
        using survey data collected in 1998 by the Center for the Study of
        Community Colleges. Chapters analyze approaches to general education,
        vocational course offerings, the liberal arts, multicultural education, ESL,
        honors programs, and distance learning.
        ISBN: 0-7879-4849-7

**NEW DIRECTIONS FOR COMMUNITY COLLEGES
IS NOW AVAILABLE ONLINE AT WILEY INTERSCIENCE**

What is Wiley InterScience?

Wiley InterScience is the dynamic online content service from John Wiley &
Sons delivering the full text of over 300 leading scientific, technical, medical,
and professional journals, plus major reference works, the acclaimed *Current
Protocols* laboratory manuals, and even the full text of select Wiley print books
online.

What are some special features of Wiley InterScience?

Wiley InterScience Alerts is a service that delivers table of contents via e-mail
for any journal available on Wiley InterScience as soon as a new issue is
published online.
Early View is Wiley's exclusive service presenting individual articles online as
soon as they are ready, even before the release of the compiled print issue.
These articles are complete, peer-reviewed, and citable.
CrossRef is the innovative multi-publisher reference linking system enabling
readers to move seamlessly from a reference in a journal article to the cited
publication, typically located on a different server and published by a different
publisher.

How can I access Wiley InterScience?

Visit http://www.interscience.wiley.com

Guest Users can browse Wiley InterScience for unrestricted access to journal
Tables of Contents and Article Abstracts, or use the powerful search engine.
Registered Users are provided with a *Personal Home Page* to store and
manage customized alerts, searches, and links to favorite journals and articles.
Additionally, Registered Users can view free Online Sample Issues and preview
selected material from major reference works.
Licensed Customers are entitled to access full-text journal articles in PDF, with
select journals also offering full-text HTML.

How do I become an Authorized User?

Authorized Users are individuals authorized by a paying Customer to have
access to the journals in Wiley InterScience. For example, a university that
subscribes to Wiley journals is considered to be the Customer. Faculty, staff and
students authorized by the university to have access to those journals in Wiley
InterScience are Authorized Users. Users should contact their Library for information on which Wiley journals they have access to in Wiley InterScience.

ASK YOUR INSTITUTION ABOUT WILEY INTERSCIENCE TODAY!

Printed in the United States
64044LVS00005B/65